OECD ECONOMIC SURVEYS

TURKEY

JUNE 1987

ORGANISATION FOR ECONOMIC CO-OPERATION AND DEVELOPMENT

Pursuant to article 1 of the Convention signed in Paris on 14th December, 1960, and which came into force on 30th September, 1961, the Organisation for Economic Co-operation and Development (OECD) shall promote policies designed:

- to achieve the highest sustainable economic growth and employment and a rising standard of living in Member countries, while maintaining financial stability, and thus to contribute to the development of the world economy;
- to contribute to sound economic expansion in Member as well as non-member countries in the process of economic development; and
- to contribute to the expansion of world trade on a multilateral, non-discriminatory basis in accordance with international obligations.

The original Member countries of the OECD are Austria, Belgium, Canada, Denmark, France, the Federal Republic of Germany, Greece, Iceland, Ireland, Italy, Luxembourg, the Netherlands, Norway, Portugal, Spain, Sweden, Switzerland, Turkey, the United Kingdom and the United States. The following countries became Members subsequently through accession at the dates indicated hereafter: Japan (28th April, 1964), Finland (28th January, 1969), Australia (7th June, 1971) and New Zealand (29th May, 1973).

The Socialist Federal Republic of Yugoslavia takes part in some of the work of the OECD (agreement of 28th October, 1961).

Publié également en français.

CONTENTS

Introduction		7
I.	**Recent trends**	8
	Demand and output	8
	The labour market	11
	Prices, wages and incomes	12
	Medium-term aspects of the interaction of wages, inflation and unemployment	16
	Foreign trade and balance of payments	17
	Medium-term export performance	26
II.	**Economic policy**	31
	Monetary policy	31
	Fiscal policy	40
III.	**Short-term forecasts**	48
IV.	**Structural adjustment in the public sector**	50
	General government accounts	51
	Fiscal reform programme	57
	Government debt	58
V.	**Conclusions**	60
Notes		62
Annexes		
I.	Nominal wages, inflation and the NAIRU	63
II.	Constant market share analysis of export growth	65
III.	Calendar of main economic events	67
Statistical annex		73

TABLES

Text

1.	Demand and output	9
2.	Gross fixed investment by sector	10
3.	Labour market	11
4.	Prices	13
5.	Wages	15
6.	Adjustment of real wage earnings	16
7.	Dollar exchange rate of the Turkish lira	19
8.	Foreign trade	20
9.	Geographic distribution of foreign trade	22
10.	Balance of payments	24

11. Classification of merchandise exports in the constant market share analysis 27
12. Constant market share analysis 30
13. Money and credit 32
14. Foreign exchange position of deposit money banks 34
15. Central Bank credits 37
16. Selected interest rates 38
17. Credits and deposits of deposit money banks 39
18. Public sector borrowing requirements 41
19. Central government budget 43
20. Central government budget revenues 44
21. Financial account of the State Economic Enterprises 46
22. Short-term forecast 48
23. General government consolidated account 51
24. General government accounts 52
25. Consolidated account of special funds 53
26. General government expenditures by spending categories 54
27. Relative shares of tax revenues 56
28. Tax elasticities 58
29. Indicators of the public debt burden 59

Statistical annex

A. National product 74
B. Supply and use of resources 75
C. Agricultural production 76
D. Industrial production 77
E. Prices 78
F. Imports by commodities 79
G. Exports by commodities 80
H. Balance of payments 81
I. Money and banking 83
J. Workers' remittances by month 84
K. Dollar exchange rate of the Turkish lira 85
L. External debt of Turkey 86

Statistics on public sector trends:

M. General government consolidated account 87
N. Central government budget 88
O. Local administrations 89
P. Social security institutions: Pension Fund, Social Insurance Agency, Bag-Kur 90
Q. Special funds: Revenues and expenditures 91

DIAGRAMS

1. Labour market developments 12
2. Breakdown of changes in the total supply deflator 14
3. Exchange rate developments 18
4. Structure of the balance of payments and foreign trade performance 23
5. Foreign debt 25
6. Geographical decomposition of export growth 28
7. Effect of product composition on export growth 29
8. Monetary indicators 36
9. Central Bank credits 40
10. Major components of tax revenues 55

BASIC STATISTICS OF TURKEY

THE LAND

Area (thousand sq. km)	781	Major cities, 1985	
Agricultural area (thousand sq. km)	280	(thousand inhabitants):	
Forests (thousand sq. km)	202	Istanbul	5 495
		Ankara	2 252
		Izmir	1 490

THE PEOPLE

Population, 1986 (thousands)	50 923	Civilian labour force, 1986 (thousands)	18 512
Per sq. km, 1986	65	Civilian employment:	15 512
Annual average rate of change		Agriculture, forestry, fishing	8 712
of population (1980-1985)	2.2	Industry	2 170
		Construction	652
		Services	3 978

PRODUCTION

GNP, 1986 (TL billion)	39 191	Origin of GDP, 1986 (per cent):	
Per head (US $)	1 148	Agriculture, forestry, fishing	16.5
Gross fixed investment, 1986		Industry	29.0
(TL billion)	5 260	Construction	3.6
Per cent of GNP	23.6	Services	50.9
Per head (US $)	27.2		

THE GOVERNMENT

Public consumption, 1986		Public debt, end-1986	
(per cent of GNP)	8.8	(per cent of GNP):	51.1
Central government current revenue,		Domestic	22.3
1986 (per cent of GNP)	17.5	Foreign	28.7

FOREIGN TRADE

Commodity exports, 1986, fob		Commodity imports, 1986, cif	
(per cent of GNP)	12.7	(per cent of GNP)	19.1
Main exports (per cent of total exports):		Main imports	
Agriculture	25.3	(per cent of total imports):	
Mining	3.3	Machinery and equipment	28.5
Industry	71.4	Transport equipment	6.9
		Base metals	11.7
		Oil	17.9

WORKERS' REMITTANCES
(US $ million)

1985	1 774	1986	1 696

THE CURRENCY

Monetary unit: Turkish lira		Currency unit per US $,	
		average of daily rates:	
		1984	363.46
		1985	519.46
		1986	669.03

Note: An international comparison of certain basic statistics is given in an annex table.

This Survey is based on the Secretariat's study prepared for the annual review of Turkey by the Economic and Development Review Committee on 15th May 1987.

•

After revisions in the light of dicussions during the review, final approval of the Survey for publication was given by the Committee on 10th June 1987.

•

The previous Survey of Turkey was issued in September 1986.

INTRODUCTION

In 1986, the Turkish economy expanded considerably faster than envisaged; GNP growth at close to 8 per cent was the highest among OECD countries. Output in agriculture and manufacturing industries was particularly buoyant. Domestic demand growth was fuelled by a vigorous expansion of both consumption and investment, whilst the contribution to growth from the foreign balance was negative. As a consequence of the weak growth of exports of goods and services and a strong rise in imports, notably of investment goods, the current account deficit rose to $1.5 billion.

Although there are signs of overheating of the economy as some sectors have reached capacity limits, inflation has been reduced, helped as in other countries by lower dollar prices of imported oil and other commodities, as well as by decelerating food prices in the wake of a good harvest and moderate increases in labour cost. Deceleration in the expansion of the monetary aggregates also seems to have contributed to damping the price rise. Employment increased somewhat more rapidly than the labour force for the first time in many years, making some inroad on high unemployment.

Economic policies have followed the strategy adopted in 1980, which aimed at reducing the influence of the State on the economy and gradually moving towards a market-determined regime of resource allocation. New measures have been introduced to simplify administration, and to further liberalise foreign trade, and capital and exchange transactions. Emphasis has also been put on the development of money and capital markets. On the fiscal policy side, greater autonomy given to local administrations has resulted in improved public services, whilst the operation of special investment funds seems to have speeded up investment in infrastructure and housing. Improvements in tax collection following the introduction of value-added tax in 1985 have helped to keep general government budget deficits in the region of 2 per cent of GNP.

Current economic trends are reviewed in Part I of the present Economic Survey. This part also contains an analysis of the interaction of wages, inflation and unemployment, and an analysis of Turkey's export performance from the mid-1970s to the middle of the 1980s. Part II presents an overview of recent monetary policy measures and their impact on money, credit and interest rates, as well as of developments in public finances. Short-term forecasts are outlined in Part III. Part IV discusses the role of the public sector in the economy and problems related to government deficits and debt. Policy conclusions are presented in Part V.

I. RECENT TRENDS

Demand and output

According to preliminary official estimates, economic growth in 1986 was significantly stronger than forecast in last year's OECD Economic Survey of Turkey. The acceleration of real GNP growth to an annual average of 8 per cent was driven by a vigorous and broadly-based upturn in domestic demand (Table 1). Imports of goods and services grew faster than predicted and the estimated negative contribution of the real foreign balance to GNP growth was –2.9 percentage points. Output in all major sectors accelerated in 1986. Industrial production, in particular, was boosted by strong growth of output in manufacturing and by an acceleration in the production of electricity. Altogether, capacity utilisation in industry is estimated to have risen further and may be near to its technical maximum in several industrial branches.

Growth of total domestic demand appears to have doubled in 1986 to 10.9 per cent. Available indicators suggest that the acceleration of activity in 1986 was stronger in the first half of the year; merchandise imports, in particular, rose rapidly, worsening the trade balance. This prompted the authorities to take measures to contain domestic demand growth and to stop the deterioration of the external balance. As a result, the upswing appears to have been somewhat more moderate in the second half of the year.

Private consumption, which accounts for about two-thirds of GNP, appears to have been the mainstay of domestic activity in 1986. Although calculated as a residual in Turkish National Accounts and therefore prone to measurement errors, it appears to have grown by nearly 10 per cent in real terms, which is the highest rate of expansion registered since 1976. The recorded strength of private consumption is somewhat surprising in so far as real wages in the private and the public sector are estimated to have been fairly flat or even falling. But employment in the non-agricultural sector rose rapidly; the effective reduction of income taxes as well as the system of tax rebates also helped, and incomes in the agricultural sector appear to have recovered due to strong output growth. Public consumption is also estimated to have accelerated its growth to 8.8 per cent in 1986.

Fixed investment was the most dynamic demand component, stimulated by high capacity utilisation and strong demand growth. Private fixed investment was particularly buoyant, growing at a rate of 13.8 per cent, i.e at nearly twice the rate achieved in the preceding year. Investment in the energy sector grew particularly rapidly but, given its small weight, contributed only little to total investment (Table 2). Housing investment expanded at an impressive rate of 31 per cent stimulated by the activities of the Housing Fund. But fixed capital formation by the manufacturing sector increased below average (6.5 per cent), whilst private agricultural investment decreased for the second consecutive year. Stronger growth of investment in manufacturing industry may be needed to avoid serious capacity bottlenecks. Private sector spokesmen have been complaining about the high level of real interest rates, but a favourable profit situation (see Diagram 2 below) as well as official investment incentives designed to direct private investment to certain sectors and regions of the country should counterbalance this effect.

Table 1. **Demand and output**

	1985 Current prices		Average volume change		Percentage volume change over previous year					
	TL billion	As per cent of GNP/GDP	1973-77	1978-80	1981	1982	1983	1984	1985	1986[1]
GNP at market prices	27 789	100.0	6.5	1.8	4.1	4.5	3.3	5.9	5.1	8.0
Foreign balance[2]	–525	1.9	–1.7	4.2	2.5	1.7	–1.3	0.3	0.6	–2.9
Exports	6 809	24.5	–3.9	14.5	47.0	24.9	9.1	20.5	10.6	3.4
Imports	7 334	26.4	7.9	–10.5	15.7	10.8	13.6	16.7	7.3	16.2
Total domestic demand	28 315	101.9	8.2	–2.4	1.6	2.8	4.7	5.4	4.4	10.9
Stockbuilding[2]	240	0.9	0.0	0.8	0.8	–1.0	0.2	0.4	–0.5	0.4
Final domestic demand	28 075	101.0	8.2	–3.2	0.8	3.7	4.3	5.0	5.0	10.5
Private investment	2 334	8.4	9.8	–11.7	–8.7	5.5	4.7	8.7	7.8	13.8
Public investment	3 228	11.6	18.4	–4.6	9.4	2.2	1.9	3.3	16.0	13.7
Private consumption	20 181	72.6	6.6	–3.1	0.6	4.2	5.0	5.1	3.0	9.7
Public consumption	2 332	8.4	9.5	6.7	0.9	2.0	1.7	3.0	3.2	8.8
GDP at factor cost	25 526	100.0	7.1	0.9	3.6	4.5	3.9	6.0	4.2	7.3
Agriculture	4 790	18.8	3.2	2.4	0.1	6.4	–0.1	3.5	2.4	7.7
Industry	8 060	31.6	9.7	–1.8	7.4	4.9	8.0	10.1	6.3	9.0
Mining	650	2.5	15.8	–1.9	–7.3	–5.5	7.5	7.9	11.9	–4.6
Manufacturing	6 409	25.1	8.8	–2.5	9.5	5.4	8.7	10.2	5.5	9.8
Energy	1 001	3.9	13.4	5.4	7.0	11.6	2.2	11.1	7.8	15.5
Construction	951	3.7	7.1	3.0	0.4	0.5	0.6	1.9	2.9	8.3
Services	11 725	45.9	8.0	1.1	4.2	3.9	4.4	5.7	4.1	6.0

1. Provisional.
2. Changes expressed as per cent of GNP in previous period.

Source: State Planning Organisation, *Main Economic Indicators.*

Table 2. **Gross fixed investment by sector**

	1985 Current prices		Percentage volume change over previous year					
	TL bill.	Share in per cent	1981	1982	1983	1984	1985	1986[1]
Private sector								
Agriculture	209.8	9.0	27.5	9.2	7.0	2.1	–17.0	–16.0
Mining	15.0	0.6	1.3	8.6	4.4	10.6	19.4	9.3
Manufacturing	766.5	32.8	–2.0	0.6	1.0	6.5	4.6	6.7
Energy[2]	13.6	0.6	6.7	3.9	5.7	12.8	–10.1	87.6
Transportation	415.3	17.8	29.0	12.8	9.3	13.8	9.2	7.5
Tourism	44.9	1.9	2.2	6.3	5.7	88.6	59.7	31.9
Housing	744.5	31.9	–34.7	4.8	5.0	9.0	17.0	30.0
Education	8.7	0.4	6.7	5.6	2.4	9.0	100.7	34.7
Health	11.4	0.5	6.0	4.3	1.7	7.1	136.1	44.8
Other services	104.0	4.5	4.4	2.2	2.6	10.1	8.2	9.2
Total	2 333.7	100.0 (42.0)	–8.7	5.5	4.7	8.7	7.8	13.8
Public sector								
Agriculture	206.3	6.4	54.6	8.0	–15.2	–5.5	–16.9	19.5
Mining	316.4	9.8	37.4	–17.4	19.4	–3.2	23.8	–35.1
Manufacturing	404.8	12.5	–8.5	–15.9	–3.3	0.7	–4.6	–20.1
Energy[2]	735.1	22.8	4.4	11.6	10.5	2.2	9.4	19.8
Transportation	933.4	28.9	6.0	16.7	5.7	7.0	37.0	25.6
Tourism	23.3	0.7	21.2	–11.3	20.6	30.9	–7.4	64.5
Housing	70.2	2.2	34.9	–27.0	0.9	45.0	0.3	–21.2
Education	124.2	3.8	22.8	22.0	–11.4	–12.4	27.4	5.8
Health	39.5	1.2	36.8	9.7	–28.0	–8.9	0.8	63.3
Other services	373.8	11.6	17.6	16.1	–5.7	18.7	41.8	54.8
Total	3 227.6	100.0 (58.0)	9.4	2.2	1.9	3.3	16.0	13.7
Total gross fixed investment	5 561.3	(100.0)	1.7	3.5	3.0	5.5	12.5	13.8

1. Provisional.
2. Electricity, gas, water.
Source: State Planning Organisation, *Main Economic Indicators.*

Public fixed capital formation also grew strongly (13.7 per cent in volume terms), but decelerated in comparison to 1985 as a result of the policy measures taken to avoid an overheating of the economy. Inter alia, State Economic Enterprises (SEE) were induced to contain their spending so that their investment declined in real terms at an estimated rate of 8.4 per cent; public investment in manufacturing and mining decreased by roughly 25 per cent. The observed decline in public investment in manufacturing industries since 1981 is a reflection of the Turkish authorities' belief that public activities should be reduced in areas which could benefit more from the free play of market forces. Declining investment activity of the SEEs in 1986 was, however, more than offset by strong investment expenditures of extra-budgetary funds and municipalities.

Manufacturing output, which accounts for about 80 per cent of industrial production, increased by 10.7 per cent in 1986. Output of the energy sector accelerated to 15½ per cent, whilst activity in mining decreased. Favourable weather conditions and some improvements in the quality of inputs led to an increase in agricultural output by 7.7 per cent, mainly due to a strong increase in cereal production; output of cotton declined. Output in construction industries rose by 8.3 per cent in 1986 in response to the favourable investment climate as well as the increased activity of the State housing fund. The services sector increased its output by an estimated 6 per cent, led by the increase of value-added in trade which expanded by some 9 per cent in real terms in 1986.

The labour market

Due to high population growth (2¼ per cent) and an even stronger increase in the active population, the reduction of unemployment is a difficult task. The Turkish authorities estimate that an annual growth of real GNP of roughly 6¼ per cent is required just to keep unemployment unchanged. In 1986, this critical growth rate was exceeded and the officially estimated rate of unemployment decreased by ¾ percentage point to 15½ per cent of the civilian labour force, the first decline in a decade (Diagram 1). It was, however, not only the acceleration in demand and output that helped to reduce the number of unemployed from 3 million in 1985 to 2.9 million in 1986. Another factor was the decline in the participation ratio, which fell to 59 per cent in 1986.

Employment in the services sector appears to have benefited most from the strength of economic activity. Employment in transportation, commerce and other services (including a small residual item) increased by some 200 000 persons, representing nearly two-thirds of the increase in total civilian employment by 329 000 persons. However, employment in industry and construction also rose rapidly, namely by 5.8 and 4.7 per cent, respectively. Only in the agricultural sector, which holds the largest share of the total labour force, did employment decrease slightly (–0.1 per cent), continuing a long-established trend. The increase in total employment by only 2.2 per cent implies an upsurge in productivity of 5 per cent after rates of 4½ and 3 per cent in 1984 and 1985, respectively. This productivity gain is the highest since 1976 and points to remarkable productivity reserves in the Turkish economy.

Table 3. **Labour market**

	1986[1] Thousand	Percentage change over previous year						
		1980	1981	1982	1983	1984	1985	1986[1]
Population	50 923	2.2	2.2	2.2	2.2	2.2	2.2	2.2
Population aged 15-64	32 465	2.9	2.9	2.9	2.9	2.9	2.8	2.7
Participation ratio (per cent)		63.1	62.3	61.5	60.8	60.0	59.4	58.8
Civilian labour force	18 512	1.4	1.4	1.4	1.4	1.4	1.4	1.3
Civilian employment	15 632	–0.1	0.9	0.6	0.7	1.3	1.1	2.1
Agriculture	8 712	–0.1	–0.1	–0.3	–0.3	–0.3	–0.2	–0.1
Industry and construction	2 822	–0.1	2.2	1.5	2.4	3.7	3.3	5.5
Services	4 098	0.6	2.8	2.7	2.4	3.7	3.3	5.4
Unemployment[2]	2 880	14.8	15.2	15.6	16.1	16.1	16.3	15.5
Unemployment excluding seasonal unemployment in agriculture	2 228	10.7	11.2	11.8	12.4	12.4	12.7	12.0
Productivity								
GDP		–0.4	2.7	3.9	3.2	4.6	3.1	5.1
Agriculture		1.8	0.2	6.7	0.3	3.8	2.7	7.8
Industry		–4.4	3.5	2.4	3.9	4.4	2.2	3.3
Services		0.2	2.5	1.2	2.1	1.8	1.3	0.6

1. Provisional.
2. As per cent of civilian labour force.
Source: State Planning Organisation, *Main Economic Indicators.*

Diagram 1. **Labour market developments**

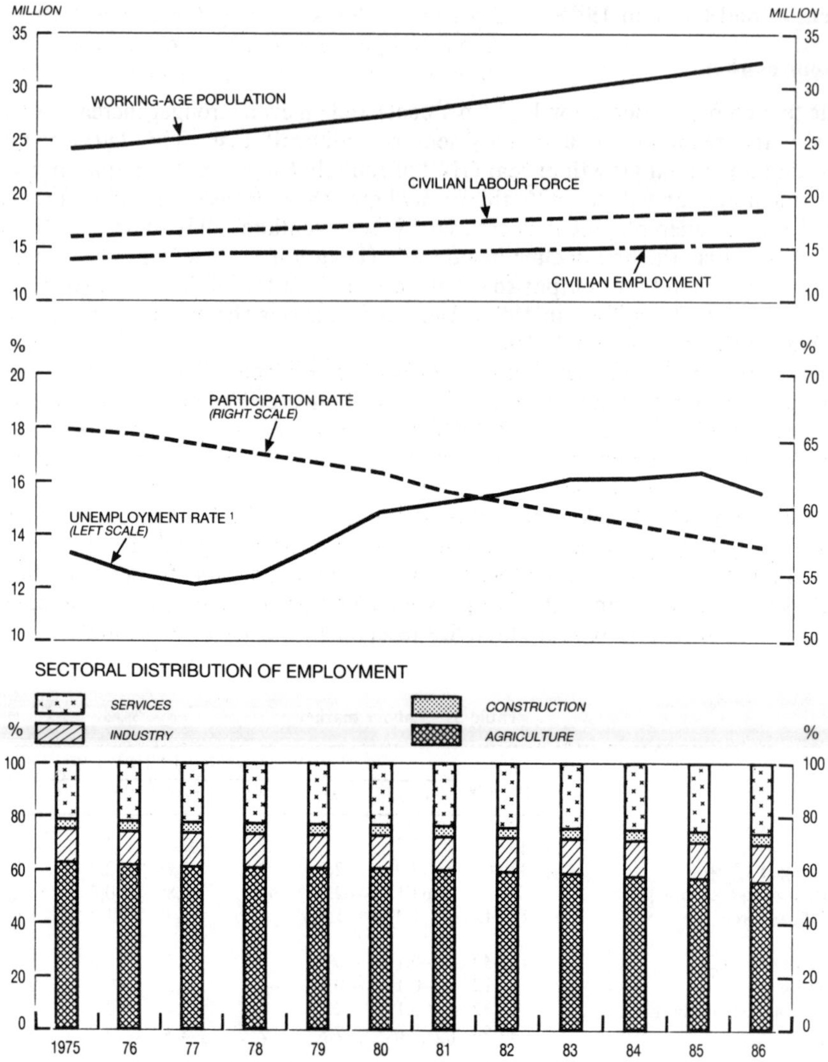

1. Seasonal unemployment in agriculture is included.
Source: Date submitted by the State Planning Organisation.

Prices, wages and incomes

As in most other OECD Member countries, favourable external influences on import prices, particularly the fall of commodity prices, have exerted a damping effect on domestic inflation. However, the Turkish policy of managed floating of the lira to maintain price competitiveness of exports limits the effect of stabilizing influences on domestic prices through the exchange rate mechanism. Indeed, since Spring 1985, when the US dollar began to depreciate *vis-à-vis* major currencies, until the end of 1986, the US dollar exchange rate of the Turkish lira fell by more than 35 per cent. However, in as far as the dollar prices of imported goods stabilize or fall, they exert a damping impact on lira prices. Hence, the fall of the dollar import prices by 14.4 per cent on average in 1986 helped to some extent to contain domestic inflation.

According to the wholesale price index of the State Institute of Statistics (SIS), the inflation rate fell to roughly 30 per cent in 1986 from 43.2 per cent in 1985 (Table 4). In the same period, the increase in the consumer price index of the SIS was reduced from 45 to around 35 per cent. However, the underlying rate of inflation fell somewhat less since the 1985 indexes were influenced by the introduction of the 10 per cent value added tax at the beginning of the year. When the effect of the VAT on the level of prices had disappeared in the course of 1985, inflation as measured by the change in the wholesale price index decelerated to a year-on-year rate of 38 per cent in the fourth quarter. One year later, in the fourth quarter of 1986, the same measure indicated an inflation rate of 26 per cent, i.e. 12 percentage points less. The downward pressure on prices stemming from external sources was reinforced by a moderation of agricultural prices as a result of the good harvest.

Table 4. **Prices**[1]

	Percentage change over previous year					Percentage change over corresponding period of previous year			
						1986			
	1982	1983	1984	1985	1986	Q 1	Q 2	Q 3	Q 4
Wholesale price indices									
UTFT (1963 = 100)									
General index	25.2	30.6	52.0	40.0	26.7	33.7	28.6	23.6	22.1
State Institute of Statistics (1981 = 100)									
General index	27.0	30.5	50.3	43.2	29.6	33.6	29.2	30.2	26.0
Agriculture	24.5	31.2	57.5	37.4	25.3	22.3	23.1	35.5	21.2
Mining	49.3	20.5	41.2	63.9	6.0	26.2	3.4	4.6	2.5
Manufacturing	26.5	31.2	46.6	41.9	32.6	37.9	33.3	30.2	29.8
Energy	45.7	25.7	75.3	97.6	35.6	71.8	33.7	26.1	21.8
Consumer price indices									
State Institute of Statistics (1978-79 = 100)									
National index	34.1	31.4	48.4	45.0	34.6	37.9	34.6	35.1	31.6

1. The State Institute of Statistics has published new price indices. The old series which were originally compiled by the Ministry of Commerce continue to be published by the Under-Secretariat of the Treasury and Foreign Trade (UTFT).
Source: State Institute of Statistics, ***Price Indices Monthly Bulletin.***

The fact that the gain on the inflation front was rather moderate, in relation to the sharp fall in world energy prices, was – apart from the managed devaluation of the Turkish lira – probably also the result of the acceleration of growth of domestic demand, the existence of long-term contracts for crude oil (whose renegotiation required time) as well as the authorities' decision not to pass lower import prices of oil on to domestic users, but to stabilize lira prices. This latter policy, however, should have a smoothing effect on domestic energy prices in the near future, even though oil prices in world energy markets have increased somewhat.

Given the difficulty involved in separating the effects of domestic developments, the depreciating exchange rate and world commodity prices on domestic inflation, the GNP deflator may serve as an alternative and more appropriate yardstick for measuring the underlying rate of inflation. The latter rose by 50 per cent in 1984, 44 per cent in 1985 and is estimated to have decelerated to about 30 per cent in 1986. Hence, it appears that in spite of the substantial increase in domestic demand further progress has been made on the domestic inflation front.

Diagram 2. **Breakdown of changes in the total supply deflator**[1]

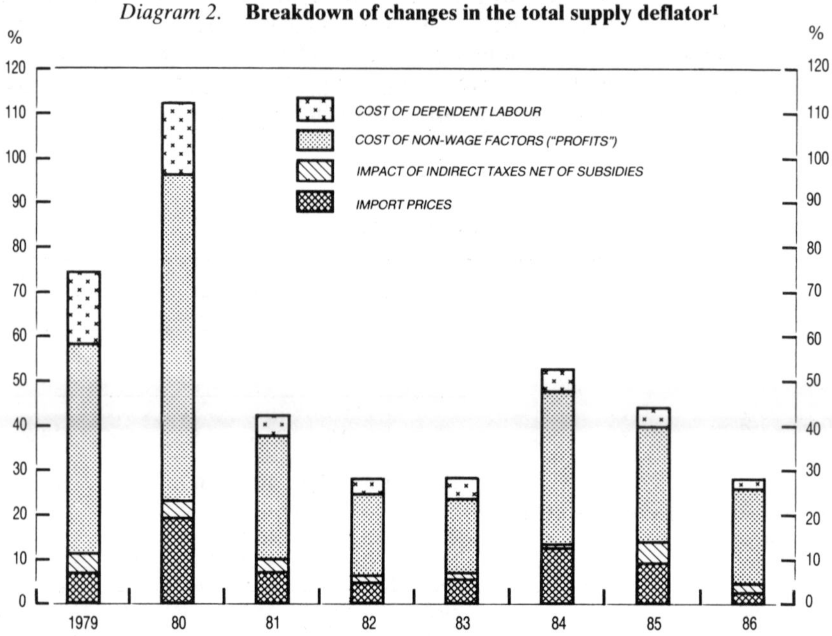

1. This diagram gives an "accounting" breakdown of the rise in prices. In no way does it seek to explain inflation in causal terms, since all the items in the breakdown are interdependent.

Source: OECD Secretariat estimates.

Another way of analysing underlying inflation is to take the total supply deflator, i.e. the deflator of the sum of GNP and imports of goods and services, and to break it down into its components. Diagram 2 shows the contribution of inputs to the change in the total supply deflator. This rather mechanical decomposition suggests that a dominant share of domestic inflation is attributable to the change in gross profit margins, whereas labour cost, import prices and net indirect taxes exerted only a relatively minor influence on domestic price changes, particularly in 1986. It has, however, to be borne in mind that the share of wages in nominal income is considerably lower than in other OECD economies. Moreover, the part of homemade inflation assigned to profits in this accounting exercise refers to a residual in nominal national income consisting of pure profits, interest incomes, other property incomes and depreciation, which together seem to have been extraordinarily buoyant over the period reviewed.

The relatively modest impact of wages on price inflation in recent years is also revealed by an inspection of nominal wage rates according to different definitions (Table 5). When doing so, it has, however, to be kept in mind that available wage statistics are very limited in coverage; there is also some doubt about their reliability. Nevertheless, it seems that nominal wage increases have decelerated sharply from 1985 to 1986 and that the average gross pay of workers and employees must be assumed to have fallen in real terms. However, due to reductions in taxation via lower tax rates and higher tax rebates, it seems likely that real disposable wage incomes have increased, which is consistent with the recorded increase in real private consumption in recent periods.

Table 5. **Wages**

	1986[1] TL per day	Percentage change over previous year					
		1981	1982	1983	1984	1985	1986[1]
Nominal wages							
Average private sector	3 414	54.8	8.7	45.1	45.2	66.1	28.6
Average public sector	4 406	61.7	28.4	34.1	46.9	43.1	29.9
Senior civil servant	10 640	46.9	59.6	24.4	77.1	72.5	46.1
Average wage level for Turkey	3 601	59.8	9.7	40.5	47.0	58.7	26.2
Legal minimum wage	1 112	117.6	1.0	50.2	66.9	86.4	0.4
Real wages[2]							
Average private sector		6.3	–14.6	11.4	1.5	14.2	–4.4
Average public sector		11.1	0.9	3.0	–4.0	–1.7	–4.1
Senior civil servant		0.9	25.4	–4.5	15.7	18.6	9.0
Average wage level for Turkey		9.8	–14.0	6.4	–4.1	9.1	–5.7
Legal minimum wage		80.8	–20.7	13.8	9.1	28.1	–25.0

1. Provisional.
2. Nominal wages deflated by the private consumption deflator.
Source: State Planning Organisation, *Annual Programmes.*

The moderate development of real wages on average over the last five years in combination with the above mentioned strong increase in labour productivity also supports the notion of favourable profitability as suggested by the decomposition of the total supply deflator. This can be inferred from the movement of the ratio of the real labour cost to the terms-of-trade adjusted labour productivity, i.e. the real wage gap, which indicates the change in the share of gross profits in nominal national income. Table 6 shows that in Turkey, in contrast to most other Member countries, where a positive real wage gap had developed over time, adjusted productivity growth has on average always outpaced the growth of real wage income. This effect was particularly pronounced in recent years and should normally be reflected in a rising trend for private investment and subsequent job creation. However, whilst total private investment has increased moderately up to 1985 and more strongly in 1986, this conclusion is somewhat at variance with the observed development of investment in manufacturing industry, which may point to the existence of structural problems and strongly uneven distribution of profits among firms, and between manufacturing and service sectors.

Table 6. **Adjustment of real wage earnings**
Compound annual growth rates

	1960-1972	1972-1979	1979-1985
Turkey[1]			
I. Real wage income	4.9	0.0	–11.9
II. Adjusted productivity	5.0	3.8	2.8
III. Real labour cost gap	–0.1	–3.8	–14.6
IV. Real labour cost	4.9	2.1	–10.2
Greece			
I. Real wage income	7.0[2]	5.7	0.7
II. Adjusted productivity	8.3	3.2	–0.3
III. Real labour cost gap	–1.2[2]	2.4	1.0
IV. Real labour cost	6.2[2]	4.8	0.8
Ireland			
I. Real wage income	4.8[2]	3.4	0.8
II. Adjusted productivity	4.9	2.6	2.5
III. Real labour cost gap	–0.1	0.8	–1.8
IV. Real labour cost	3.9	4.0	1.7
Portugal			
I. Real wage income	7.7	3.9	–2.6
II. Adjusted productivity	6.5	1.8	0.2
III. Real labour cost gap	1.2	1.4	–2.8
IV. Real labour cost	7.0	5.5	–1.8
Spain			
I. Real wage income	7.7	4.8	0.8
II. Adjusted productivity	6.8	3.9	3.3
III. Real labour cost gap	1.0	0.9	–2.5
IV. Real labour cost	7.4	4.7	1.3

Note: The variables above are defined as:
I. Total compensation per dependent employment divided by the private consumption deflator;
II. Real GNP per dependent employment adjusted for the terms of trade;
III. Real labour cost gap equals I minus II;
IV. Total compensation per dependent employment divided by the GDP deflator.
1. Dependent employment represents only about one-third of total employment in Turkey.
2. 1961-1972.
Source: OECD Secretariat estimates.

Medium-term aspects of the interaction of wages, inflation and unemployment

Although the rate of inflation as measured by wholesale and consumer price indices fell in the course of 1985 and 1986, the deceleration was less marked than in most other OECD Member countries. Hence, domestic inflationary pressures appear to persist which could lead to an acceleration of the inflation rate once the stabilizing effects of the fall in oil and other raw material prices have run their course. Therefore, it is of interest to analyse the main domestic influences on inflation in Turkey, and how these are likely to affect inflation prospects.

Experience in other OECD countries has shown that nominal wage inflation is a crucial component of price inflation in the short run. To assess how wages will develop in future and thus fuel inflation requires knowledge about the macroeconomic wage formation process. This is also important in order to judge whether there is any short- or long-run trade-off between inflation and employment. A widely accepted approach to an empirical analysis of the wage formation process consists of estimating an expectations-augmented Phillips curve, i.e. to explain changes in the wage rate by the level or variation of the rate of unemployment and expected inflation and a vector of other relevant variables. Such an analysis sheds light on the forces at work in the transformation of an economy from an inflationary to a less inflationary regime. It may also allow the calculation of an unemployment rate consistent with stable inflation. Although statistics on wages and salaries in Turkey are limited in coverage and may be biased for a variety of reasons, such as under-reporting of «true» wages paid to the social security organisation and the exclusion of most «casual» workers, who seem to make up a large part of the work force in small businesses, an attempt has been made to identify such a standard wage equation (cf. Annex I). The econometric analysis indicates that the examined wage inflation is related significantly to the level of the unemployment rate. The implication is that, if unemployment is reduced, wage inflation will increase and vice versa.

Nominal wages may also respond to expected inflation. If proxied by a moving average of past inflation rates, however, the estimates for Turkey indicate that wage growth reflects only about 20 per cent of the changes in consumer price inflation. This inertia in nominal wages seems to indicate that wages in Turkey tend to follow, rather than lead, price developments. It also implies that *real* wages appear cyclically highly flexible.

In the medium to long term, wage developments, inflation and inflation expectations must be considered to be endogenous. Given the estimated price equation, the unemployment rate consistent with stable inflation and inflation expectations – the NAIRU – can then be estimated. On the basis of a cost mark-up price equation, which also incorporates the change in import prices and a demand pressure variable, the non-accelerating inflation rate of unemployment for Turkey is estimated to be near 8 per cent. Hence, as in other OECD countries, the present unemployment rate of 12 per cent (excluding seasonal unemployment in agriculture) is well above the estimated NAIRU, which seems to indicate that the net demand effect on wage growth is currently negative and likely to stay so even if unemployment rates were lowered substantially. It has, however, to be borne in mind that the confidence interval around the NAIRU-estimate is likely to be large reflecting imprecise coefficient estimates and mis-specification in the wage and price equations. Therefore, the estimate can only be a very rough guide as to when inflationary pressures from the labour market may be expected to arise.

The fact that inflation, on the basis of present policies and in the presence of relatively high rates of unemployment, appears to be rather sticky suggests that there may be an inflation threshold, below which it may be very difficult to descend. Although there is no reason to doubt that sufficiently restrictive monetary and fiscal policy could further reduce relatively high inflation rates, this may turn out to be very costly in terms of output foregone and high unemployment. Such a threshold seems to be related to structural properties of the economy such as lack of adequate domestic and international competition, over-regulation and rigidities related to business practices. These properties were described in some detail in the 1985 Economic Survey of Turkey. Hence, it would seem advisable to supplement traditional anti-inflationary policy, such as monetary and fiscal tightening, with structural policies aimed at improving the price mechanisms and the transparency of markets.

Foreign trade and balance of payments

The new approach to trade policy

The promotion of exports and the liberalisation of imports and capital flows are key elements of the structural adjustment programme adopted in 1980. A devaluation and managed float of the Turkish lira was designed to correct over-valuation of the currency and to ensure external competitiveness on a sustained basis. Incentive schemes, which directly or

Diagram 3. **Exchange rate developments**[1]

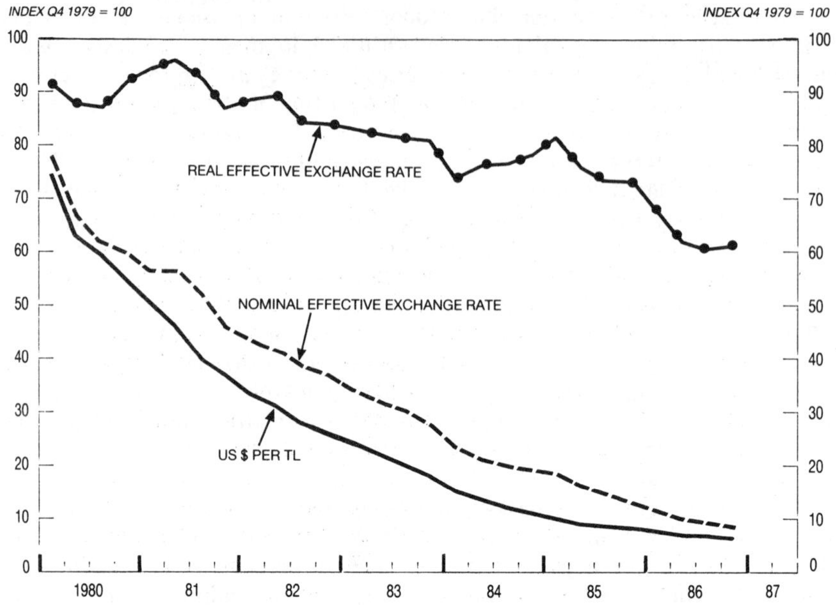

1. Monthly averages of daily figures.
Sources: OECD, *Main Economic Indicators;* OECD Secretariat estimates.

indirectly subsidised exports, were introduced, such as rebates on indirect and direct taxes paid by exporting firms, preferential export credits and allocation of foreign exchange for duty-free imports by exporters. This strategy was modified in 1984 when a gradual phasing out of tax rebates and other export subsidies was announced and the decision was taken to promote exports principally through more market-oriented mechanisms, such as a competitive exchange rate and investment incentives.

The exchange rate policy adopted in 1980 is designed to ensure that the inflation differential between Turkey and its most important trading partners would not entail an appreciation of the exchange rate in real terms. In fact, so long as the current account is in deficit a real devaluation of the lira is aimed at, in order to improve price competitiveness of exports. This approach led to a real effective depreciation – based on relative consumer price indexes in the absence of other reliable data – of the Turkish lira between 1980 and 1985 of 20 per cent. The attempted smooth downward trend in the real external value of the lira was, however, interrupted in 1984, when the rapid acceleration of domestic inflation implied a real effective appreciation in spite of nominal depreciation (Diagram 3). This has since been rectified, and between the end of 1985 and the end of 1986 the lira depreciated in real effective terms by 16 per cent. However, the lira depreciated against the dollar in the same period by only 22 per cent in nominal terms (Table 7), which implies a bilateral real appreciation of the lira *vis-à-vis* the dollar of more than 5 percentage points.

During the first half of the 1980s, this new exchange rate and trade policy was successful. Sales to almost all important regions of the world picked up vigorously and sizeable gains in

Table 7. **Dollar exchange rate of the Turkish lira**

	TL per $	Percentage change over previous period
Annual averages		
1978	24.04	–25.8
1979	37.53	–35.9
1980	76.04	–50.6
1981	110.24	–31.0
1982	160.94	–31.5
1983	224.03	–28.2
1984	363.85	–38.6
1985	519.61	–29.8
1986	669.40	–22.4
Quarterly averages		
1985		
Q 1	468.33	–10.4
Q 2	516.52	–9.3
Q 3	535.91	–3.6
Q 4	556.53	–3.7
1986		
Q 1	598.93	–7.1
Q 2	666.38	–10.1
Q 3	676.76	–1.5
Q 4	733.96	–7.8
1987		
Q 1	761.30	–3.6

Source: Central Bank of Turkey, *Monthly Statistics.*

new markets, notably in the Middle East, were achieved. The latter region's share in Turkish exports increased from about 10 percent in 1980 to above 30 per cent in 1986. Moreover, there was a noticeable shift from exports of unprocessed products to manufactured merchandise.

Trade flows

In 1986, the trade balance was influenced by two main factors. First, the oil price slide, whilst reducing Turkey's oil bill, undermined the Middle East countries' ability to import; and second, the upsurge in domestic demand stimulated imports. With demand from OECD countries being also rather subdued in contrast to the period between 1980 and 1985, exports in $ terms actually declined in 1986. In addition, Turkish exports were subject to trade restrictions in several markets. Among them, restrictions on Turkish textile exports under the Multifibre Arrangement were the most significant in quantitative terms; they affected trade between Turkey and the European Community and the United States. But there were also quantitative restrictions on certain agricultural exports from Turkey to the European Community and countervailing duties on a number of products exported to the United States. Hence, Turkish exports overall experienced a serious set-back and, in spite of the considerably lower oil bill, the trade deficit deteriorated in 1986.

When it became clear in the course of 1986 that exports were sluggish, a modified system of export premium payments was reintroduced in December, which reversed the trend towards abolition of non-market mechanisms. Preferential export credits were also brought back. The

Table 8. **Foreign trade**[1]

	1985 ($ million)	1986 ($ million)	1980	1981	1982	1983	1984	1985	1986
			Percentage change over previous year						
Exports (fob)									
Agriculture	1 719	1 886	24.4	32.8	–3.5	–12.2	–7.0	–1.7	9.7
Mining and quarrying	244	247	44.2	1.3	–9.4	8.0	26.9	1.7	1.2
Manufacturing	5 995	5 324	33.4	118.6	49.8	6.7	40.6	16.5	–11.2
Total	7 958	7 457	28.7	61.6	22.2	–0.3	24.5	11.6	–6.3
Volume			25.0	68.7	24.1	13.9	23.1	10.0	0.1
Average value			3.0	–4.2	–1.5	–12.5	1.2	1.5	–6.4
Imports (cif)									
Oil	3 612	2 008	125.6	0.4	–3.4	–2.2	–0.8	–0.7	–44.4
Industrial products	7 052	8 302	19.8	22.2	–0.1	11.2	22.9	9.6	17.7
Other	949	889	36.7	77.3	12.5	–13.1	104.1	–1.2	30.7
Total	11 613	11 199	56.0	12.9	–1.0	4.4	16.5	8.0	–3.6
Volume			52.9	11.6	10.0	12.1	18.9	7.6	12.7
Average value			2.0	1.2	–10.0	–6.9	–2.0	0.3	–14.1
			Percentage distribution						
Exports (fob)			100.0	100.0	100.0	100.0	100.0	100.0	100.0
Agriculture			57.5	47.2	37.3	32.8	24.5	21.6	25.3
Mining and quarrying			6.5	4.1	3.0	3.3	3.4	3.1	3.3
Manufacturing			36.0	48.7	59.7	63.9	72.1	75.3	71.4
Imports (cif)			100.0	100.0	100.0	100.0	100.0	100.0	100.0
Oil			48.8	43.4	42.4	39.7	33.8	31.1	17.9
Industrial products			48.7	52.7	53.2	56.7	59.8	60.7	74.1
Other			2.5	3.9	4.4	3.6	6.4	8.2	8.0

1. Excluding transit trade.

Source: State Institute of Statistics, *Monthly Indicators.*

Turkish authorities have stated, however, that these measures are only of a temporary nature. Efforts to liberalise imports were continued and quantitative restrictions were discarded to a large extent. Levies on certain categories of imports, which had been introduced in 1984, were, however, expanded between 1984 and 1986 so that quantitative import restrictions were in part replaced by import duties.

Total export volume appears to have stagnated in 1986 for the first time in six years (Table 8). This was caused by a steep fall in exports of manufactured products while exports of agricultural goods and mining and quarrying products fared better. The increase in agricultural exports signalled a halt to their decline over the preceding four years. Export prices (in US dollars) are estimated to have decreased by 6.4 per cent, a development related to the weakness in world commodity prices and the fact that Turkey is largely a price-taker in world markets. As a result, the dollar value of total exports declined by 6.3 per cent in 1986.

As mentioned above, exports to OPEC countries have suffered from the fall in their oil revenues (Table 9). Moreover, the Gulf war seems to have severely affected the foreign exchange reserves of Iran and Iraq, the two most important trading partners of Turkey in the Middle East, so that sales (in US dollars) to these two countries fell by about 45 per cent in 1986. Exports to Saudi Arabia were also weak in 1986 (– 17 per cent). Nevertheless, regional trade statistics indicate that Turkish exports to Gulf countries fell less in value terms than oil imports, so that overall the regional balance was in surplus for the first time. Exports to OECD countries in dollar values appear to have increased by 4.5 per cent in 1986. Among them, exports to the European Economic Community displayed a relatively weak picture (+1.9 per cent). Sales to France and Italy, however, appear to have risen considerably (+ 39 and + 15 per cent, respectively) whilst exports to the United Kingdom suffered a sharp fall (– 38 per cent).

In response to the upturn of domestic demand, Turkish imports overall continued to grow in real terms in 1986 (12.7 per cent). Imports of capital goods increased particularly rapidly, especially in the first half of the year, mirroring the rise of investment demand. Consumer goods imports, however, are reported to have stagnated in real terms.

Dollar import prices are estimated to have fallen by around 14.4 per cent in 1986, entailing a fall in nominal imports by 3.6 per cent. Evidently, the oil price decline accounted for the major part of the fall in import prices and lowered the oil bill by more than $1.5 billion. Hence, the increase of imports of industrial and other products by about $1 billion in 1986 was more than compensated for by cheaper oil imports.

The current account

The 1986 trade account is reported to have been in deficit by $3.1 billion (fob basis), i.e. slightly higher than in 1985 (Table 10). A counterpart to the traditional trade deficit is a surplus on the services and transfer account (Diagram 4), which mainly stems from personal remittances by Turkish workers, and from tourism. Expatriate remittances expressed in dollars, however, have been on a downward trend for a number of years. Since a considerable part of the workers' remittances are denominated in European currencies, whose external value vis-à-vis the dollar rose in 1986, the reported dollar figure conceals a stronger decrease in local currencies. This decline reflects to a considerable extent the weakness in labour markets in host countries. The statistics may, however, be misleading in so far as Turkish workers living abroad are increasingly making use of the possibility of opening foreign exchange deposits in Turkish banks; this has led to recording the workers' remittances in the short-term capital account of the balance of payments rather than in the transfers account.

Table 9. **Geographic distribution of foreign trade**[1]

$ million

	Imports (cif)						Exports(fob)					
	1986	In per cent of total					1986	In per cent of total				
		1982	1983	1984	1985	1986		1982	1983	1984	1985	1986
OECD countries	7 303	50.1	48.5	51.7	56.1	65.2	4 292	44.5	48.2	52.4	51.6	57.6
EEC countries	4 565	25.6	28.1	27.6	31.3	40.8	3 263	30.5	35.1	38.3	39.4	43.8
of which:												
France	545	3.0	2.4	2.3	4.5	1.9	299	3.4	3.2	2.8	2.7	4.0
Germany	1 772	11.4	11.4	10.9	12.1	16.0	1 444	12.3	14.6	17.9	17.5	19.4
Italy	866	4.7	5.5	5.8	5.8	7.8	580	5.7	7.4	7.0	6.3	7.8
United Kingdom	520	4.9	4.8	4.1	4.1	4.7	334	3.3	4.3	3.7	6.8	4.5
Other OECD countries	2 738	19.2	20.4	24.0	24.8	24.3	1 029	13.9	13.1	14.1	12.2	13.8
of which:												
Japan	684	4.0	3.8	3.8	4.5	6.2	99	0.7	0.6	0.5	0.5	1.3
Switzerland	285	3.5	2.9	2.2	1.6	2.6	162	5.6	5.0	5.0	1.6	2.2
United States	1 177	9.2	7.5	10.0	10.1	10.6	549	4.4	4.1	5.2	6.4	7.4
Eastern Bloc	872	4.8	8.7	8.8	5.7	7.8	311	5.6	4.3	4.0	4.2	4.2
of which:												
Soviet Union	353	1.2	2.6	2.9	1.9	3.2	141	2.2	1.1	2.0	2.4	1.9
Middle East and North Africa	2 041	41.9	36.7	36.2	33.0	18.2	2 578	45.0	41.1	42.0	42.8	34.6
of which:												
Algeria	32	0.1	0.8	1.0	1.4	0.3	177	2.2	2.2	1.8	1.4	2.4
Egypt	17	0.0	0.3	0.0	0.0	0.2	145	2.5	1.2	2.0	1.8	1.9
Iran	221	8.5	13.2	14.4	11.2	2.0	564	13.8	19.0	10.5	13.6	7.6
Iraq	769	16.0	10.3	8.8	10.0	6.9	553	10.6	5.6	13.1	12.1	7.4
Jordan	10	0.1	0.1	0.0	0.1	0.1	169	1.8	1.9	1.5	1.4	2.3
Kuwait	209	11.0	1.8	0.9	0.9	1.9	121	1.5	1.5	1.5	1.5	1.6
Lebanon	6	0.1	0.0	0.0	0.0	0.1	136	1.9	2.1	1.4	1.1	1.8
Libya	292	10.4	8.6	6.1	5.5	2.6	136	4.1	3.2	2.0	0.7	1.8
Saudi Arabia	176	5.4	2.9	2.0	2.0	1.6	357	6.2	6.3	5.3	5.4	4.8
Syria	19	0.2	0.0	0.2	0.1	0.2	62	1.1	1.0	0.9	0.7	0.8
Other countries	983	3.2	6.1	3.3	5.2	8.8	276	4.9	6.4	1.6	1.4	3.6
Total	11 199	100.0	100.0	100.0	100.0	100.0	7 457	100.0	100.0	100.0	100.0	100.0

1. Excluding transit trade.
Source: State Institute of Statistics, *Monthly Indicators*.

Diagram 4. **Structure of the balance of payments and foreign trade performance**

Per cent of GNP

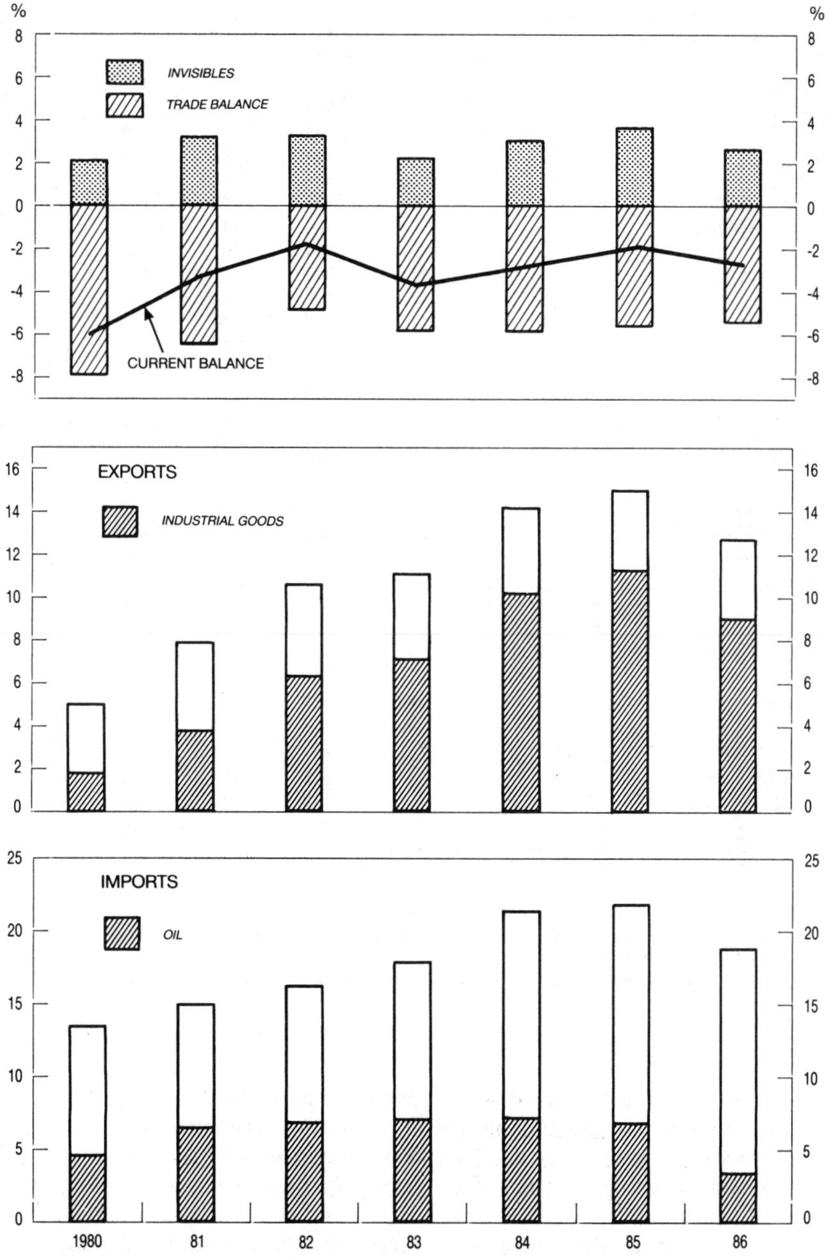

Source: State Planning Organisation, *Main Economic Indicators*.

Table 10. **Balance of payments**

$ million

	1982	1983	1984	1985	1986*
Trade balance[1]	–2 628	–2 990	–2 942	–2 975	–3 081
Exports (fob)	5 890	5 905	7 389	8 255	7 583
Imports (fob)	8 518	8 895	10 331	11 230	10 664
Invisibles, net	1 793	1 162	1 535	1 962	1 553
Services	–501	–623	–579	–36	–396
Tourism	224	292	271	770	637
Investment income	–1 372	–1 379	–1 387	–1 321	–1 664
Interest payments	–1 464	–1 441	–1 586	–1 753	–2 134
Other	92	62	199	432	470
Other services	647	464	537	515	631
Transfers	2 294	1 785	2 114	1 998	1 949
Official[2]	105	236	229	236	246
Private	2 189	1 549	1 885	1 762	1 703
Workers' remittances	2 140	1 513	1 807	1 714	1 634
Other[3]	49	36	78	48	69
Current balance	–835	–1 828	–1 407	–1 013	–1 528
Long-term capital, net	984	279	1 159	75	650
Direct investment	55	46	113	98	125
Credits received	1 882	1 299	2 150	1 835	2 670
Project credits	754	508	733	926	1 296
Other official credits[4]	982	535	873	280	723
Private credits	146	256	544	629	651
Debt repayments	–953	–1 066	–1 104	–1 858	–2 145
Official	–953	–998	–969	–1 711	–1 735
Private	–	–68	–135	–147	–410
Basic balance	149	–1 549	–248	–938	–878
Short-term capital	81	1 033	36	1 656	1 478
Errors and omissions	–75	507	317	–818	–65
Counterpart items	13	161	–171	223	251
Overall balance	168	152	–66	123	786
Change in official reserves	–168	–152	66	–123	–786
Net use of IMF	133	112	–141	–103	–241
Other	–301	–264	207	–20	–545

* Provisional.
1. Including transit trade.
2. Including grants.
3. Including workers' imports.
4. Including European Resettlement Fund loans, World Bank Structural Adjustment loans and bilateral programme loans.

Source: Central Bank of Turkey, *Monthly Statistics.*

Net receipts from tourism were on an upward trend in the first half of the 1980s as a result of investment in tourism and successful marketing. The surplus shrank, however, in 1986 when gross tourism receipts declined as a consequence of the fall in the number of American tourists travelling overseas, and a strong increase in prices of services following a successful 1985 season.

Income from other services, of which a large part stems from construction services of Turkish building contractors abroad, also continued to rise in 1986. On the debit side of the services account, expenditure continued to rise as a result of the increase in interest payments on external debt, its biggest item (Table 10). In sum, although the invisibles balance remained in surplus, it was about $400 million lower than a year before, thus widening the estimated deficit in the current account of the balance of payments from $1 billion in 1985 to $1.5 billion in 1986. In per cent of GNP the current account deficit rose from 1.9 per cent in 1985 to 2.6 per cent in 1986.

The capital account and external debt

The surplus in the capital balance increased by an estimated $600 million in 1986, mainly due to an inflow of long-term capital to the non-bank sector. Direct investment, although being on a comparatively low level, increased, too. The net inflow of short-term capital was somewhat below the level recorded in 1985.

The continuing deficits in the current account of the balance of payments lead to a rising stock of external debt which *ceteris paribus* induces rising debt service payments. Higher interest payments, in turn, contribute to a deterioration of the current balance. Between 1980 and 1986, the level of external debt as a share in GNP rose from 27.8 to 53.3 per cent (Diagram 5). However, the increase in external indebtedness expressed in dollars in 1986 is also a result of the fall in the dollar exchange rate which inflated the dollar value of liabilities denominated in other currencies. The effect of this can be put at about $2 1/2 billion in 1986. Short-term debt rose considerably in this period, reaching a share in total outstanding debt of roughly one-fifth. This increase in short-term liabilities was to a considerable extent caused by borrowing of the private sector, as banks have increasingly made use of the possibilities created for trade financing following the liberalisation of capital movements since 1984.

Diagram 5. **Foreign debt**
Per cent of GNP

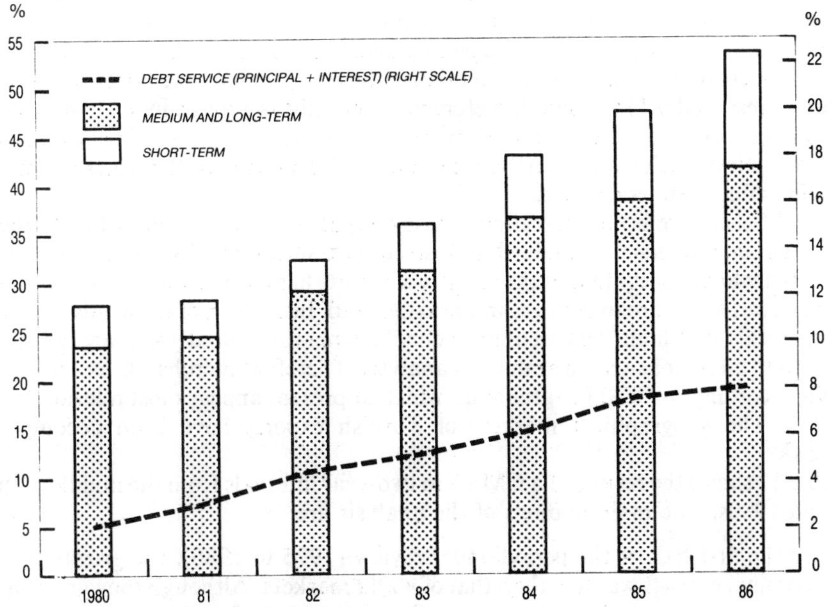

Source: Central Bank of Turkey, *Annual Reports*.

Debt service payments increased rapidly, from $1.5 billion in 1980 to an estimated $4.3 billion in 1986. In the same period, the ratio of debt service payments to export earnings rose from 22.4 per cent to 36.1 per cent, but this figure also reflects the recent weakening of exports.

Medium-term export performance

Given that in the medium to long run the balance of payments imposes a serious constraint on a country aiming to grow faster than most of its trading partners, Turkish growth possibilities are to a large extent dependent upon the country's export performance. As has been pointed out, particular emphasis has been placed by the Turkish authorities on policies which are designed to develop a competitive external sector. As a result, Turkish merchandise exports grew at impressive rates in the early 1980s, but displayed some signs of weakness in 1986. Hence, the question may be asked as to how far the structural adjustment programme has enhanced the international competitiveness of exporting industries.

One way of examining the Turkish export performance over the medium term is to make use of the Constant Market Share Analysis (CMSA)[1]. It decomposes the growth differential between world exports and exports of a particular country into the following three components:

- The effect due to the geographical composition of the export market;
- The effect due to the product bundle exported (the items where the country enjoys a comparative advantage);
- A residual term.

Preferably, the analysis should be made using volume data which would better justify considering the residual term as a measure of competitiveness. However, data limitations impose the choice of value data (US dollars). Unfortunately, given floating exchange rates and relatively rapid inflation, using dollar value terms for world exports and exports of a particular country is likely to distort the picture and, as a result, the residual term includes not only the competitiveness effect, but also other influences, such as exchange rate swings, etc. The figures presented below should therefore be taken only as a rough indication of the volume effects on Turkey's exports resulting from relative export price changes *vis-à-vis* its competitors. Nevertheless, the analysis remains valid as far as the market and product competition effects are concerned.

It would also have been interesting to disaggregate export data according to the OECD Secretariat's International Standard Industrial Classification (ISIC) in order to gauge whether the technology content of the country's exports has changed significantly over time to adapt the export structure to changes in world demand. Inspection of the available trade data, however, reveals that high- and medium-technology manufactured goods are not sufficiently represented to allow for such an ambitious analysis. Therefore merchandise export data have been split according to 18 SITC-groupings which at present appear most relevant for Turkey (Table 11). The geographical markets of Turkish exports have been decomposed into 16 regions[2].

Table 12 shows the results of a CMSA in two-year intervals from the middle of the 1970s to the mid-1980s. The main findings of the analysis are:

- In the first half of the period under review (1975 to 1980), the growth of Turkey's nominal exports was less than that of world markets. Although they grew on average at a rate of more than 10 per cent, Turkish exports failed to keep up with rapidly expanding world demand in that period. In the first half of the 1980s, however, when

Table 11. **Classification of merchandise exports in the constant market share analysis**

Number in diagram 7	Commodity group	SITC category (2nd revision)
1	Meat	011
2	Cereals	041, 043, 046
3	Vegetables and fruit	05
4	Sugar and honey	061
5	Tobacco (non-manufactured)	121
6	Other food, beverages and other tobacco	Other 0, 1
7	Cotton, synthetic fibres, wool	263, 266, 268
8	Crude minerals	278
9	Other crude materials, animal and vegetable oils, fats and waxes	Other 2, 4
10	Petroleum products (refined)	334
11	Textile yarn, fabrics and made-up articles	651, 652, 653, 658, 659
12	Lime, cement and fabricated construction materials	661
13	Glass and glassware	664, 665
14	Iron and steel	671, 672, 673, 674, 678
15	Electrical equipment and machinery	773, 775, 778
16	Road vehicles	781, 783, 784
17	Articles of apparel and clothing accessories	84
18	All other products	Other 3, 5, 6, 7, 8, 9

Source: OECD, *Foreign Trade by Commodities*, 1985.

world market growth slowed sharply, Turkish exports continued to rise at two-digit rates and hence exceeded significantly the expansion of world markets;

- The commodity composition effect exerted in most cases a negative influence on export performance, although some improvement has been registered recently;
- The market destination effect (i.e. the difference between the growth of Turkish regional export markets and that of world trade) was positive in the period ending in 1983, displaying particular strength in 1980-82, when Turkish exporters benefited from strong spending of Middle-East oil-producing countries in the wake of the second oil-price hike. This is also corroborated by Diagram 6 which shows that Turkish exports to most of its OECD trading partners (panel a) and to OPEC countries (panel b) were winning market shares in increasing as well as in declining regional markets. The two-yearly CMSA, however, reveals that in recent years the regional market effect turned negative, which may to a large extent reflect payments problems of OPEC countries due to the fall in oil prices.
- The residual component, i.e. the "competitiveness effect", was negative in the first half of the sample period, but was large and positive in the first half of the 1980s, and hence accounts for the better part of the positive growth differential between Turkey's exports and world imports.

Diagram 7 seeks to present a more detailed picture of the commodity composition of merchandise exports over time. Product groups are assigned numbers according to Table 11. The essential message of the different panels of Diagram 7 is that the number of products which gained shares in expanding markets has increased over time; moreover, shares have also been gained in shrinking markets (goods categories which are placed on the right hand side of the 45° line). Since the commodity composition of Turkish exports has been identified by the

Diagram 6. **Geographical decomposition of export growth**

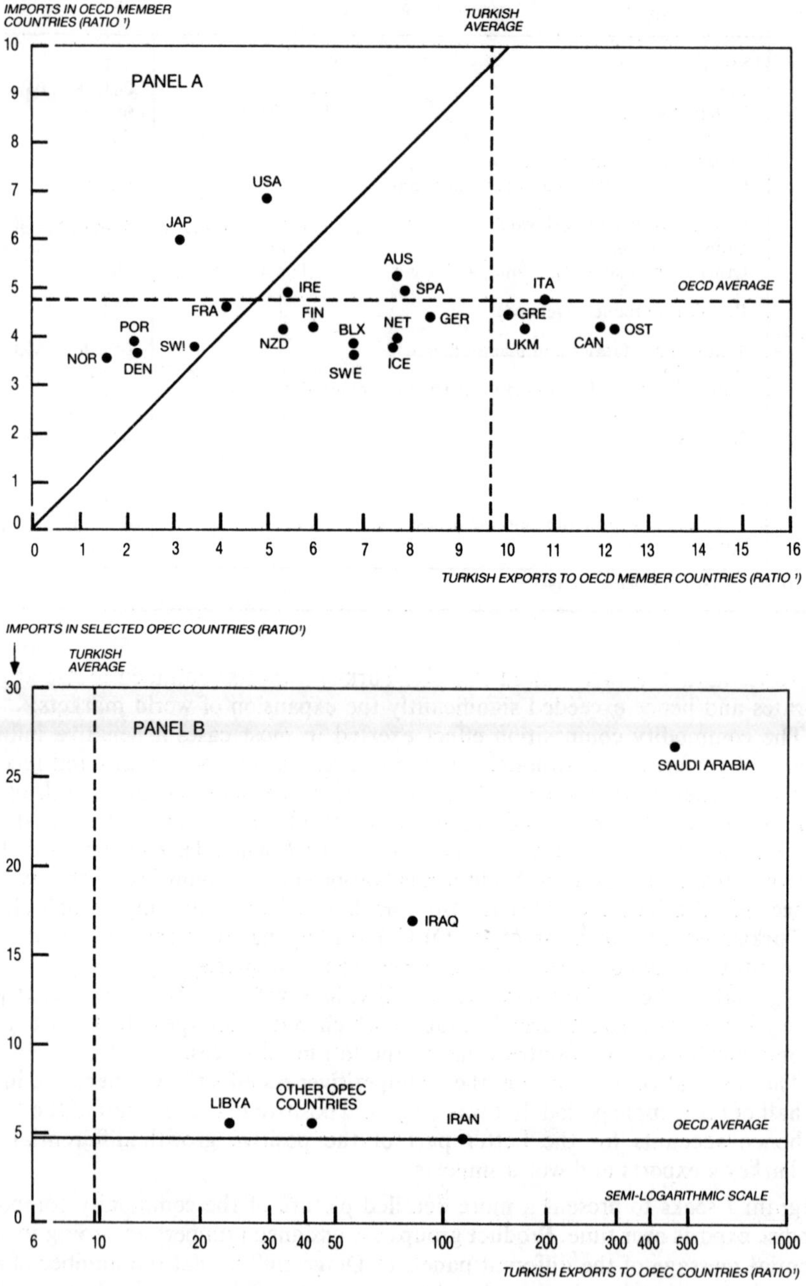

1. Ratio of the average value of imports (exports) 1984-1985 to the average value 1971-1972.
Source: OECD Secretariat calculations based on OECD, *Foreign Trade by Commodities*, 1985.

Diagram 7. **Effect of product composition on export growth**[1]

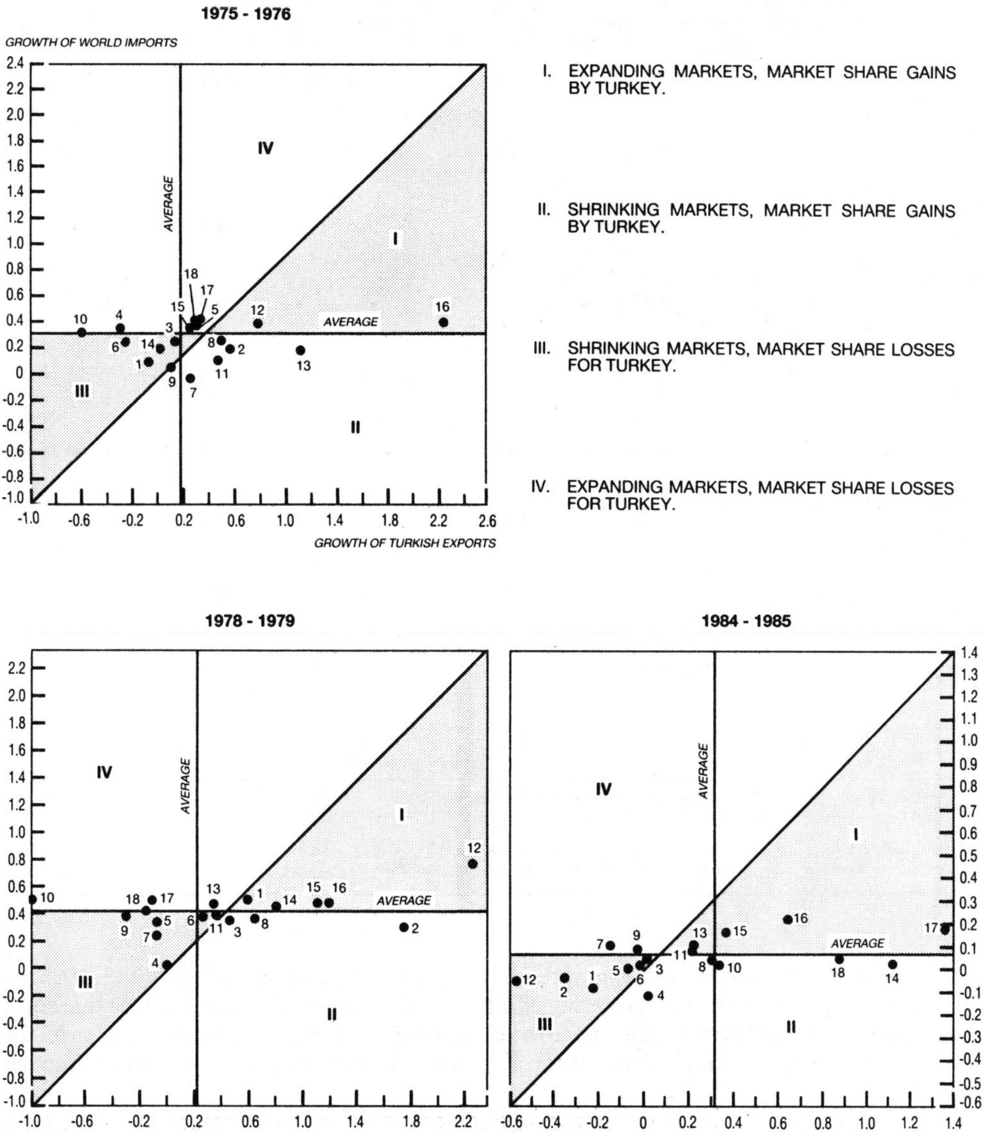

1. For the definition of products 1 to 18, see Table 11.

Source: OECD Secretariat calculations based on OECD, *Foreign Trade by Commodities*, 1985.

Table 12. **Constant market share analysis**[1]

Per cent

	Growth of Turkish merchandise exports	Growth of world merchandise exports	Difference	Regional composition effect[2]	Product mix effect[3]	Residual
1975-76 / 1973-74	8.5	14.6	-6.1	6.2	-6.4	-7.2
1976-77 / 1974-75	12.5	10.9	1.6	2.3	-0.4	-0.3
1977-78 / 1975-76	9.7	14.6	-4.9	0.5	-1.4	-4.7
1978-79 / 1976-77	10.7	19.0	-8.3	1.5	-3.0	-8.4
1979-80 / 1977-78	13.1	22.3	-9.2	3.3	-6.4	-8.4
1980-81 / 1978-79	29.4	14.8	14.6	11.3	-5.4	10.5
1981-82 / 1979-80	42.1	1.2	42.5	9.6	-0.9	34.6
1982-83 / 1980-81	22.8	-4.7	27.5	0.5	0.8	25.5
1983-84 / 1981-82	11.0	-1.5	12.5	-0.9	0.4	12.7
1984-85 / 1982-83	14.7	3.7	11.3	-4.1	-0.1	15.3

1. Data refer to annual growth rates in value of exports. Statistical discrepancies are due to rounding.
2. The regional composition effect measures the differential in export growth rates resulting from the geographical pattern of Turkish export markets.
3. The product mix effect measures the differential in export growth rates resulting from the product mix of Turkish exports.

Source: OECD Secretariat calculations based on OECD, *Foreign Trade by Commodities,* 1985.

CMSA as relatively unfavourable, it appears that price competitiveness has been improving relative to competitors, or that marketing efforts have been relatively successful, or that some other unidentified positive factors have been at work (e.g. export subsidies). Hence the interpretation of the residual factor of the Constant Market Share Analysis merits further attention.

It is particularly noteworthy that the residual term turns out to be negative for the 1970s, the period when the lira was considerably overvalued, and that it takes on a positive value in recent periods after the lira exchange rate depreciated. Relating the residual of the CMSA to a real effective exchange rate – in the absence of a reliable series for relative unit labour cost relative consumer price indices in common currency have been used – it turns out that there is a statistically significant negative correlation between the two variables; the price competitiveness, as measured by the real exchange rate defined above, explains 70 per cent of the variation of the residual of the CMSA[3].

II. ECONOMIC POLICY

Monetary policy

According to the monetarist school of economic thought, inflation over the medium to long run is primarily a monetary phenomenon. But even economists who do not adhere to this view are likely to concede that – no matter what may trigger inflation originally, e.g. demand pressures in product markets or exogenous price shocks such as changes in import prices or taxes – excessive growth in the supply of money is a necessary condition for inflationary pressures to persist in the longer run. Hence, in a country such as Turkey, where high inflation has been a major problem and an impediment to balanced economic growth, monetary policy is of focal interest.

This was clearly recognised by the Turkish authorities in 1980, when the structural reform programme was designed. As a first measure, positive real interest rates were introduced, which can be considered as an intermediate target of monetary policy. However, the fact that the Central Bank of Turkey shares responsibility for monetary policy with other government institutions and that it was obliged to fund selective credit programmes and the public sector in general, made effective control of monetary aggregates extremely difficult, if not impossible. Therefore further reforms of the monetary system and of monetary control instruments were needed and have been introduced in recent years.

The reserve and liquidity requirement system was overhauled in 1985 and 1986. A unified required reserve ratio of 21 per cent was introduced in March 1985 and reduced in several steps to 15 per cent in March 1986. Interest paid on lira bank reserves was gradually reduced to zero by January 1986. In the absence of counter-measures, the reduction of reserve ratios would have boosted monetary aggregates via an increase of the reserve money multiplier. Therefore the Central Bank obliged commercial banks to keep the reserves thus freed with the Central Bank as an advance on future reserve growth or to invest them in Treasury paper. Banks are also compelled to keep 15 per cent of their deposits as eligible liquid reserves. Since October 1986, 3 per cent of deposits have to be kept in cash and free reserves and 12 per cent in the form of unused rediscount quota and government securities.

Commercial banks' operations in foreign currency have expanded rapidly since the liberalisation measures taken in 1983. To control the growth of foreign exchange deposits of residents and non-residents, required reserves on these deposits of 20 per cent held with the Central Bank were imposed in January 1986. Following a liquidity crisis experienced by some banks, the ratio was lowered to 15 per cent in March 1986 so that the same reserve requirement ratio now applies to domestic and foreign currency deposits. The cost to commercial banks are, however, different since lira reserves earn no interest while foreign currency reserves earn interest following the rates in the Euromarket. On top of the reserve requirements, foreign exchange assets and liabilities are subject to a variety of other ratio requirements such as a liquidity ratio on short-term liabilities and off-balance sheet contingent liabilities in the form of liquid foreign assets, an exchange rate risk ratio and a utilisation ratio.

Table 13. **Money and credit**

End of period:	1985 December TL bill.	1980	1981	1982	1983	1984	1985	1986[1] Q 1	1986[1] Q 2	1986[1] Q 3	1986[1] Q 4
		Percentage change over corresponding period of previous year									
Currency in circulation	1 011	54.2	33.6	45.8	32.8	32.5	37.5	47.6	42.4	47.6	42.9
Sight deposits	2 197	51.4	42.2	34.6	49.9	8.9	44.8	41.0	50.0	47.0	66.7
M1	3 208	58.2	38.1	38.0	44.6	16.1	43.2	43.7	46.8	47.3	57.2
Time deposits	4 937	114.5	273.9	82.3	11.2	117.2	68.7	64.2	33.4	23.9	12.7
M2	8 145	66.8	85.8	56.0	28.7	57.4	57.3	45.0	38.2	32.3	38.8
M2X	9 316	..	..	..	..	66.9	62.5	61.8	53.8	51.0	55.0
Domestic credits[2]	7 115	66.6	55.2	32.5	28.5	35.9	68.1	64.3	74.2	73.9	68.1
by: Deposit money banks	5 552	76.9	67.0	36.5	33.8	38.9	76.8	80.8	91.3	92.1	76.7
Investment banks	646	24.4	45.2	40.8	23.9	25.0	20.7	19.1	37.5	45.2	64.4
Central Bank	917	71.9	34.6	17.8	12.7	31.6	35.5	38.2	30.1	21.1	28.7
to : Treasury	794	105.8	38.8	24.4	27.2	56.0	50.4	38.4	27.6	23.4	23.7
Public enterprises	1 145	44.3	26.2	17.1	12.9	0.1	112.4	..	..	..	..
Private sector	5 176	74.0	78.7	41.2	34.5	44.4	63.6	..	..	..	..
		Percentage distribution									
Domestic credits[2]		100.0	100.0	100.0	100.0	100.0	100.0	100.0	100.0	100.0	100.0
by: Deposit money banks		59.5	64.1	66.0	70.3	71.8	78.0	74.4	77.4	77.9	78.2
Investment banks		12.7	11.9	12.6	12.4	11.5	9.1	10.4	9.8	9.5	10.3
Central Bank		27.8	24.0	21.4	17.3	16.7	12.9	15.2	12.7	12.6	11.5
to : Treasury		14.2	12.7	11.9	9.9	11.6	11.2	14.9	14.9	11.0	9.8
Public enterprises		33.8	27.5	24.9	21.8	16.0	16.1	..	..	..	..
Private sector		52.0	59.8	63.2	68.3	72.4	72.7	..	..	..	..

1. Provisional.
2. Percentage changes are adjusted for Central Bank consolidated credits of TL 60.7 billion in November 1982 and TL 423.8 billion in December 1984.

Source: Central Bank of Turkey, *Monthly Statistics*.

In April 1986, the Central Bank set up an Interbank market for one- and two-week maturities and introduced overnight transactions in May 1986. Interest rates in this market vary considerably within short periods and give a valuable indication to the Central Bank about the tightness of bank liquidity. Attempts have also been undertaken to establish an efficiently functioning secondary market for government securities. Interest rates in the Interbank market and in the secondary market for government securities are freely determined.

The development of new financial instruments is also being encouraged. A new stock exchange has been established in Istanbul in order to stimulate equity issues. In the medium term, financing instruments in the capital market could help consolidate the structure of credit of the private sector. Although the volume of the market is fairly thin so far, it may grow rapidly once the privatisation of State Economic Enterprises is under way.

In 1986, the Central Bank introduced for the first time the policy approach of targeting a monetary aggregate. Money in a wider sense (M2) was selected to be kept on a growth path during the year. The growth target was derived from projections for real income growth, inflation and interest rates. On the basis of an expected real growth of GNP of 5 per cent and inflation as measured by the wholesale price index of 25 per cent, an increase of M2 by 35 per cent was planned for 1986. Since it is not feasible to control M2 directly, the Bank derived from the target path of M2 a required growth path of reserve money and its components on the basis of projections for the reserve money multiplier over time. Data for the envisaged target for 1986, however, were not published by the Central Bank since it was felt that instruments for monetary control had to be developed further. This, of course, reduced to a considerable extent the effectiveness of the approach.

The outcome for M2 in 1986 was a growth of 38.6 per cent at the end of the year, which was close to the target set and which seems an encouraging result as it implies a considerable deceleration of the so defined monetary expansion compared to 1985 (Table 13). A further slowdown of the growth of M2 to 30 per cent is planned for 1987. This is deemed consistent with a projected real GNP growth of 5 per cent and an increase in wholesale prices of 20 per cent in 1987.

To relate monetary developments reliably to changes in real economic variables and to apply systematic targeting of a monetary aggregate, however, requires the existence of a identifiable and stable money demand function. Otherwise, i.e. if there is evidence of instability in the demand for money, a steadily growing money supply, instead of stabilizing economic activity, could well induce fluctuations and destabilize expectations. Estimates for Turkey made by the OECD Secretariat of various forms of money demand equations of the standard Goldfeld-specification cast some doubt on the validity of the assumption of M2 stability. It was easier to find an equation for M1 with satisfactory test statistics.

The instability in M2 may in part be connected to the rapid growth of foreign exchange transactions in recent years (Table 14). In the wake of the liberalisation measures adopted in 1983, substitution of lira by foreign currency even in domestic transactions is favoured by lower and fewer levies on foreign exchange than on lira transactions. Foreign currency deposits earn attractive interest rates and are not subject to withholding tax. Foreign exchange credits are either fully exempt from interest surcharges or subject to lower rates.

Foreign exchange deposits with deposit money banks have expanded from $83 million at the end of 1983 to more than $3 billion at the end of 1986 representing potential supplementary liquidity of more than 20 per cent of M2. In order to cover this potential liquidity, a broader monetary aggregate M2X has been defined which includes foreign exchange deposits. Looking at the so defined money, monetary expansion has decelerated

Table 14. **Foreign exchange position of deposit money banks**

$ million

	1983	1984	1985				1986			
			March	June	September	December	March	June	September	December
Foreign exchange assets	909	2 921	2 935	3 129	3 628	3 648	3 187	3 119	3 619	4 156
Foreign exchange holdings	849	1 860	1 706	1 753	2 015	1 595	1 222	1 151	1 531	1 819
Deposits with Central Bank	5	481	682	657	775	1 040	960	802	756	820
Foreign exchange credits	55	580	547	719	838	1 013	1 005	1 166	1 332	1 517
Foreign exchange liabilities[1]	1 294	3 335	3 427	4 119	4 713	5 254	6 002	6 387	7 023	7 481
Foreign exchange deposits[2]	83	1 180	1 212	1 576	1 606	2 061	2 343	2 677	3 120	3 437
Trade financing and other short-term liabilities[1]	1 181	1 965	2 047	2 327	3 013	3 048	3 302	3 322	3 510	3 620
Long-term liabilities	30	190	168	216	94	145	357	388	393	424
Memorandum items:										
Foreign exchange deposits in banking system	1 980	3 019	3 081	3 552	3 924	4 756	5 300	5 805	6 676	7 442
Deposits with deposit money banks[2]	83	1 180	1 212	1 576	1 606	2 061	2 343	2 677	3 120	3 436
CTLDs	647	61	37	32	25	18	17	14	10	6
Dresdner Bank deposits[3]	1 250	1 778	1 832	1 944	2 293	2 687	2 940	3 114	3 546	4 000

1. Including off-balance sheet contingent liabilities.
2. Held almost entirely by residents and emigrants.
3. At Central Bank of Turkey.

Source: Central Bank of Turkey, *Monthly Statistics*.

much less than the conventionally defined M2 (Table 13). Having grown in 1985 by 60 per cent, M2X only decelerated to 55 per cent in 1986, possibly indicating a substantial inflationary potential. However, the introduction of reserve requirements on foreign currency deposits in October 1986 may eventually slow down the expansion of foreign exchange deposits and dampen the rapid increase in M2X. As there are clear signs of substitution of foreign currency for Turkish lira, it appears advisable to monitor the development of M2X closely and possibly to choose this aggregate for monetary targeting purposes rather than M2.

Since 1979, the ratio of reserve money to money in a broader sense (M2), i.e. the reserve money multiplier, has been – with some interruptions – on a rising trend, which means that small increases in reserve money have led to relatively large rises in M2 (Diagram 8). This upward trend was in part an effect of the declining share of currency in circulation in M2 ensuing from high interest rates on time deposits, and also reflects the reduction of the required reserve ratio; it is probably also a result of increased efficiency of the commercial banks' use of reserve money. The growth of reserve money decelerated from 42 per cent at the end of 1985 to 27 per cent by end-1986, following slower credit expansion in the public and in the private sector (Table 15) and a sharp increase in net foreign assets. Since the correlation of reserve money growth with inflation appears relatively close, this may give rise to hopes for further success at the inflation front.

Due to the trend increase in the reserve multiplier, the slowing pace in the growth of reserve money did not translate into a similar deceleration in the expansion of M2. Hence, after an annual average growth of 50 per cent in 1984 it accelerated to 61 per cent in 1985 and decelerated to about 37 per cent in 1986. There were, however, signs of renewed acceleration of M2 at the end of 1986 and at the beginning of 1987. On the basis of the estimated nominal GNP in 1986, the average income elasticity of M2 remained roughly constant in 1986. Owing to a shift of funds out of time deposits into sight deposits reflecting changes in relative interest rates, M1 accelerated somewhat in 1986, particularly at the end of the year (Table 13).

Given the strength of domestic demand in recent periods and the high rate of inflation, official policy is aimed at maintaining positive real interest rates in order to promote savings and discourage excessive consumer expenditures. This policy has been implemented by the Central Bank through the setting of its own lending rates and the deposit rates of commercial banks. Nominal interest rates were adjusted in line with decelerating inflation in 1985 and 1986, thus leaving the real after-tax deposit rates for three to twelve months' maturities at a level above 10 per cent. In October 1986, a first step was taken to liberalise deposit interest rates. Since then, banks have been allowed to pay interest on minimum balances of sight deposits up to 90 per cent of the prevailing time deposit rate. This step was undertaken to make lira sight deposits more attractive versus foreign currency sight deposits, which bear market interest rates. Foreign exchange deposit rates fell in 1985, but seem to have remained stable in 1986, thus entailing a rise in real interest earnings from these deposits.

A number of taxes and levies influence effective interest rates and distort the interest rates' function as indicators of the scarcity of capital. Among them is a withholding tax on deposit interest earnings which is at present equal to 10 per cent. Since 1986, an extra 3 per cent of this withholding tax has to be paid to the Defence Industry Support Fund which raised the effective withholding tax to 10.3 per cent.

Lending rates of commercial banks as well as the Central Bank remained largely unchanged from mid-1985 into late 1986 (Table 16). Lending rates are set freely by commercial banks and are at present in the order of 10 per cent above rates on time deposits of one year maturity. Front-end fees and other charges are added to this. The extremely high interest margins of banks reveal the high cost of financial intermediation which appears in

Diagram 8. **Monetary indicators**

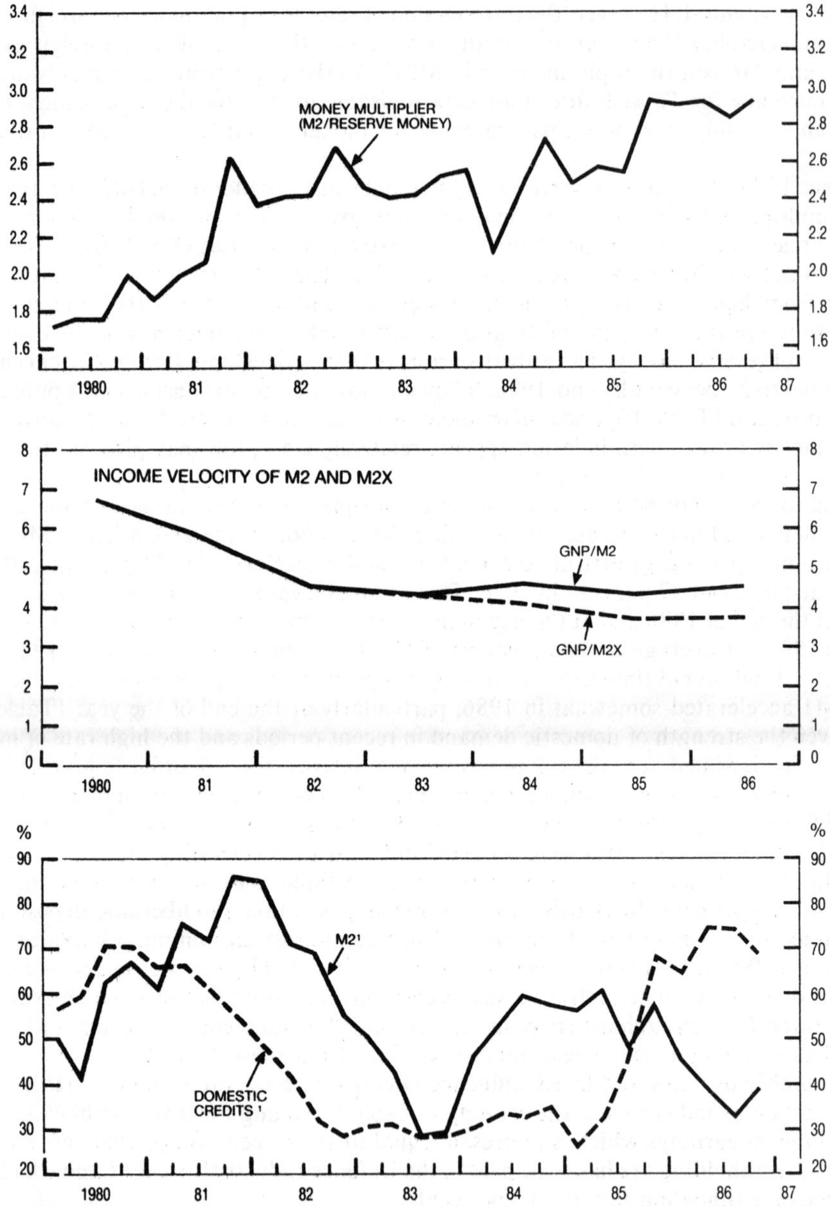

1. Percentage change over corresponding quarter of previous year.
Source: Central Bank of Turkey, *Monthly Indicators.*

Table 15. **Central Bank credits**[1]

End of period:	1985 TL billion	Percentage change over corresponding period of previous year									
		1980	1981	1982	1983	1984	1985	1986[2]			
								Q 1	Q 2	Q 3	Q 4
Credits to public sector	916.9	71.9	34.6	17.8	12.7	31.6	62.2	38.3	30.2	21.0	28.7
Advances to the Treasury	794.5	105.8	38.8	24.4	27.2	56.0	50.3	38.4	39.7	23.4	23.8
Public enterprises	122.4	44.7	30.9	9.9	–1.6	–1.0	231.7	35.2	17.6	5.8	68.0
Credits to banking system	382.7	71.4	49.3	–10.0	66.2	–18.0	21.6	12.6	21.4	47.4	25.3
Credits to deposit money banks[3]	333.0	98.4	57.1	–14.7	77.2	–22.1	19.7	7.9	23.6	50.8	12.6
Others	49.7	2.1	10.6	24.7	13.0	14.7	36.5	29.4	12.6	36.4	111.3
Total credits	1 299.6	71.5	41.2	4.9	33.4	8.2	47.7	31.4	27.4	27.6	36.1

1. Percentage changes are adjusted for Central Bank consolidated credits of TL 60.7 billion in November 1982 and TL 423.8 billion in December 1984.
2. Provisional.
3. Including credits to agricultural co-operatives.

Source: Central Bank of Turkey, *Monthly Statistics.*

Table 16. **Selected interest rates**

Per cent per annum

Central Bank	1983		1984		1985		1986	1987
	1.1.	1.7.	1.1.	14.5.	1.1.	1.3.	1.11.	24.1.
Short-terme credits								
General	31½	31½	48½	52	52	52	48	45
Agricultural credits								
Credit co-operatives	18	18	25	25	28	28	28	28
Sales co-operatives	16¼	16¼	37	37	46½	46½	46½	45
Small tradesmen and artisans	15½	15½	23	23	27	27	27	27
Export credits	31½	30	35[1]	42[1]	52	52	38	35
Support purchases for SEEs	13½	13½	21½	21½	21½	30	30	30
Medium-terme credits	33	29½	50½	50½	50½	50½	50½	48½

Commercial banks	1984			1985		1986				1987	
	1.3.	14.5.	15.8.	1.7.	1.8.	1.3.	1.5.	1.7.	1.11.	1.1.	9.2.
Deposit rates											
Sight deposits	5	5	5	5	5	5	11⅔	10	10[3]	10[3]	10[3]
Time deposits[2]											
1 month	43	35	35	35	35	35	35	30	29	28	28
3 months	49	52	53	48	45	44	42	40	36	35	35
6 months	47	48	52	52	50	48	45	45	41	39	38
1 year	45	45	45	56	55	55	52	52	48	45	43
Lending rates[4]											
Short-term credits											
General		55		62			60				
Agriculture		28		30			30				
Export		45		60			55				
Medium-term credits											
General		50		62			58				
Agriculture		16		31			31				
Long-term credits											
General		58		60			58				
Government bonds		59		56			50				

1. Increased to 35 per cent on 19.12.1983, to 40 per cent on 1.3.1984, and to 45 per cent on 7.7.1984.
2. 4 percentage points more for deposits by workers abroad.
3. Minimum rate, negotiable between the bank and the depositor for a higher rate.
4. Estimated average annual rates.

Source: Central Bank of Turkey, *Monthly Statistics*.

part to be caused by inefficiencies of the banking system. There is, however, a great variety of lending rates and there are also indications that average lending rates are lower than those published by banks.

Non-preferential lending by commercial banks is subject to a system of bank commission, financial transaction tax, a surcharge for the Resource Utilisation Fund and a stamp duty, which adds about 10 percentage points to the level of lending rates. Preferential credit rates, subsidised through special rediscount facilities at the Central Bank, are granted for investment in agriculture, small businesses and housing. The availability of preferential credits as well as the degree of subsidisation of their interest rates has been lowered in recent years, which is revealed by the declining share of bank credit refinanced at the Central Bank from nearly 30 per cent at the end of 1980 to about 13 per cent in 1985. Against the background of weakening exports, the Central Bank re-introduced preferential export credits in the autumn of 1986.

Whilst credit expansion in Turkish lira is estimated to have decelerated from 1985 to 1986, it was, however, still growing strongly (Table 17). The volume of credit extended by the Central Bank declined in the early 1980s, thus mirroring the aim of the authorities to reduce the importance of preferential credit schemes and to promote the role of commercial banks in the process of financial intermediation. In recent years, however, Central Bank credit – in

Table 17. **Credits and deposits of deposit money banks**

End of period:	1985 TL bill.	1980	1981	1982	1983	1984	1985	1986[1]
		Percentage change over previous year						
Total credits[2]	5 567	76.9	67.0	36.5	33.8	38.9	76.8	76.7
of which:								
Agricultural sales co-operatives	342	63.2	94.2	7.2	22.0	–23.2	141.0	
Other agricultural credits	613	92.0	70.7	47.4	77.9	18.7	58.2	
Manufacturing	1 580	68.0	66.5	23.0	–3.6	64.1	89.7	
Construction	594	5.8	125.4	69.1	84.0	92.7	137.6	
Exports	718	165.0	116.9	304.5	44.3	2.5	28.0	
Imports	259	46.8	86.0	90.0	–21.1	197.2	90.0	
Other claims	2 065	86.4	73.5	86.6	20.8	157.4	109.6	41.6
Government bonds	1 426	96.4	96.2	74.0	10.6	226.3	215.4	41.7
Others[3]	639	76.2	32.8	118.9	43.9	32.2	97.2	41.5
Total claims	7 632	77.4	67.4	41.6	32.2	53.1	84.6	65.5
Total deposits	7 999	68.0	102.5	56.2	30.8	61.5	60.5	29.9
		Ratios						
Credits/deposits		105.9	87.4	76.6	78.4	67.5	69.6	73.9
Total claims/deposits		117.1	96.9	87.9	88.8	84.3	95.4	105.9
Central Bank rediscount credits/total credits		30.4	28.5	17.8	23.5	8.8	12.8	5.7
Legal reserves with the Central Bank/deposits		18.4	15.7	17.0	18.2	20.0	17.2	14.2

1. Provisional.
2. Percentage changes are adjusted for Central Bank consolidated credits of TL 60.7 billion in November 1982 and TL 423.8 billion in December 1984.
3. Equity participation and private bonds.
Source: Central Bank of Turkey, *Monthly Statistics*.

Diagram 9. **Central Bank credits**

Percentage change over corresponding quarter of previous year

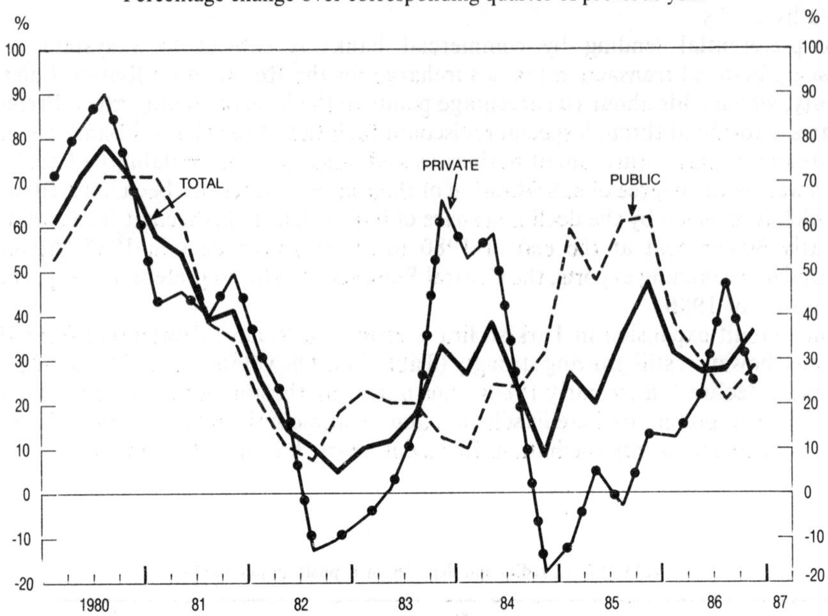

Source: Central Bank of Turkey, *Monthly Indicators.*

particular credit extended to the private sector – has been rising again (Diagram 9). Apart from the rapid expansion of lira credits, commercial banks also increasingly extended foreign currency credits. From the end of 1983 to end-1986, the ratio of foreign to local currency credits of deposit money banks rose from about 1 per cent to 12 per cent.

Fiscal policy

General government

Turkey's public sector borrowing (excluding State Economic Enterprises) related to GNP appears small by international comparison. When SEEs are included in the total public sector deficit, however, the picture changes considerably (Table 18). General government expenditure (central and local government, social security institutions and special funds) averaged 25 per cent of GNP in 1984-1985; preliminary estimates for 1986 point to an increase to 27.3 per cent. Similarly, general government revenues, which were 21 percent of GNP in 1984, rose to 23 per cent in 1985 and are estimated to have reached a ratio to GNP of 25 per cent in 1986. Thus, the general government deficit has increased to about 2.3 per cent of GNP (1½ per cent in 1985). Hence, there may be some reason for concern in respect of the potential deficit over the medium run.

Table 18. **Public sector borrowing requirements**

	1970	1975	1980	1981	1982	1983	1984	1985	1986[1]
General government deficit (TL billion)	–0.8	6.0	–149.8	–49.4	–142.3	–217.1	–692.5	–420.2	–888.8
Per cent of GNP	–0.5	1.1	–3.4	–0.8	–1.6	–1.9	–3.8	–1.5	–2.3
Total public sector deficit including SEEs (TL billion)	–3.8	–1.0	–444.8	–355.4	–487.3	–552.1	–1 200.5	–1 270.2	–2 383.1
Per cent of GNP	–2.6	–0.1	–10.0	–5.4	–5.6	–4.8	–6.6	–4.6	–6.1
Sources of borrowing (per cent of total)									
Foreign borrowing, net	..	..	19.3	41.4	18.4	42.6	56.8	16.0	53.3
Domestic borrowing, net[2]	..	46.9	46.3	38.6	68.6	45.6	27.7	63.4	35.9
Central Bank	..	..	34.4	20.0	13.0.	11.8	15.3	20.6	10.8

1. Provisional.
2. Including short-term borrowing and arrears.

Source: Data submitted by the State Planning Organisation.

Furthermore, a potential loss in fiscal flexibility may result from the declining share of the central government in general government operations, ensuing from the expansion of special funds and the growing importance of local government expenditure for infrastructure investment purposes. Since the pace of this process of decentralisation appears to have been more rapid than initially intended, measures were introduced in 1986 to slow it down. In particular, previous plans to raise the share of local administrations in total tax revenues further were cancelled.

Central government

Although the initial target of a balanced budget could not be achieved, the central government budget deficit as a percentage of GNP was nearly halved to 2.8 per cent in 1985 (Table 19). This favourable result was due less to increased discipline on the expenditure side of the budget, than to buoyant tax revenues, notably a surge in indirect tax receipts following the introduction of value added tax (VAT) in January 1985. For 1986, a further reduction in the central government budget deficit to 1.6 per cent relative to GNP had been planned. However, largely due to a strong increase in investment expenditure and transfer payments, the outcome of the central government borrowing requirement is estimated to be of the order of 3.2 per cent of GNP as against 2.8 per cent in 1985.

In nominal terms, total expenditures of the central government are estimated to have increased by 54.1 per cent in 1986, resulting *inter alia* from an increase of interest payments by 81.7 per cent and a rise of investment expenditure of 63.2 per cent. The central government wage and salary bill increased by 43 per cent and the growth in transfers to State Economic Enterprises (SEE) was lower, which implies a fall in real terms of the latter in 1986. When the surge in public investment expenditure became apparent in the course of 1986, steps were taken by the authorities to restrict spending growth by a cut in budget appropriations for expenditures other than wages and salaries and interest payments in the second half of 1986.

As in the previous year, central government revenues rose considerably faster than nominal GNP. This was again mainly the result of a vigorous increase in receipts from value added tax, but also of the corporate income tax (Table 20). Evidently, the growth of revenues benefited from the unexpectedly sharp increase in domestic demand in 1986. In addition, VAT collection has been made more efficient in the second year of its existence, leading to an increase in collections of more than 80 per cent at largely unchanged tax rates. Revenues from personal income tax grew by 60.8 per cent in 1986, despite a lowering of marginal tax. Corporate income tax rose from TL 448 billion in 1985 to TL 930 billion in 1986 as a result of an increase in the tax rate from 40 to 46 per cent and the introduction of advance payments of tax. Most of this increase stemmed from higher tax payments by SEEs.

For 1987, central government revenues and expenditures are again assumed to rise faster than nominal GNP, the latter being projected to grow at a rate of about 26 per cent. Current estimates for 1987 foresee an increase in revenues by 47.7 per cent and growth of expenditures of 43.6 per cent, thus reducing the budget deficit to 2.9 per cent of GNP. It is assumed that the recent trend of improved efficiency of the tax collection system will persist and should, together with some rate increases in less important taxes and the introduction of advance income tax payments, boost tax revenues. Advances on income taxes are, in principle, paid at a rate of 50 per cent of VAT payments by businesses and the self-employed. Revenues from VAT are expected to rise by 52.7 per cent in 1987. In December 1986, the standard value added tax rate was increased by 2 percentage points to 12 per cent and special rates of 5 per cent and 1 per cent were introduced on certain products. The zero rate on basic foodstuffs, however, was maintained.

Table 19. **Central government budget**
TL billion[1]

	1983	1984	1985	1986	1987 Current estimate	Percentage change over previous year 1986/85	1987/86
Revenues	2 314	2 840	4 476	6 851	10 120	53.4	47.6
Tax revenues	1 934	2 372	3 829	5 991	8 860	55.3	47.9
Non-tax revenues	380	468	647	860	1 260	40.1	45.3
Expenditures	2 612	3 784	5 263	8 101	11 643	54.1	43.6
Personnel expenditures	671	925	1 275	1 823	2 400	43.0	31.7
Other current expenditures	391	559	811	1 206	1 600	48.7	32.7
Interest payments	181	375	595	1 081	2 806	81.7	67.1
Foreign borrowing	130	264	427	682	1 006	59.7	47.5
Domestic borrowing	51	111	168	399	800	137.5	100.5
Investment	478	688	989	1 614	2 366	63.2	46.6
Transfers to SEEs	292	275	181	138	430	–23.8	211.6
Other transfers	570	896	1 333	2 246	3 041	59.1	35.4
Budget balance	–298	–944	–787	–1 257	–1 523		
Change in accounts payable, net	131	–56	–74	–170	–		
Cash balance	–167	–1 000	–861	–1 427	–1 523		
Financing							
Foreign borrowing	–91	333	–223	–140	–568		
Receipts from loans	59	569	197	624	572		
Payments on loans	–150	–236	–420	–764	–1 140		
Domestic borrowing	160	137	498	724	1 130		
Receipts from loans	199	195	670	1 517	2 080		
Payments on loans	–30	–58	–172	–793	–950		
Central Bank	72	190	266	257	270		
Treasury bills, net	–98	284	244	668	630		
Other	115	56	76	–82	61		
Memorandum items (per cent of GNP)							
Revenues	20.0	15.5	16.1	17.5	19.6[2]		
Tax revenues	16.7	12.9	13.8	15.3	17.2[2]		
Expenditures	22.6	20.6	19.0	20.7	22.5[2]		
Budget balance	–2.6	–5.1	–2.8	–3.2	–2.9[2]		
Cash balance	–2.6	–5.4	–3.1	–3.6	–2.9[2]		
Debt service (principal + interest)	3.1	3.6	4.3	6.7	7.5[2]		
of which:							
Foreign	2.4	2.7	4.0	3.7	4.2[2]		

1. From 1983 on, the fiscal year and the calendar year coincide.
2. GNP growth 5 per cent, GNP deflator 20 per cent.
Source: Data submitted by the State Planning Organisation.

The most dynamically growing expenditure categories are projected to be the central government wage and salary bill and interest payments. Transfers to SEEs are expected to rise because of a government decision to increase their capital. To curb growth of expenditures, investment is planned to rise by 47 per cent in 1987, which implies a deceleration compared to 1986. This will be achieved by postponing the implementation of projects agreed in principle and reviewing the priorities of the medium-term investment programme.

Table 20. **Central government budget revenues**

New classification[1]

TL billion

	1984	1985	1986	1987 Current estimate	Percentage change over previous year 1986/85	1987/86
Taxes on income	1 341	1 772	3 059	4 240	72.6	38.6
Personal income tax	1 069	1 324	2 129	2 940	60.8	38.1
Corporate income tax	272	448	930	1 300	107.6	39.8
Taxes on wealth	41	54	54	90	0.0	66.7
Real estate tax	26	30	–	–	–	–
Motor vehicles tax	9	17	44	80	158.8	81.8
Inheritance and gift tax	6	7	10	10	42.8	0.0
Taxes on goods and services	602	1 098	1 850	2 820	68.5	52.4
Domestic value added tax (VAT)	175	567	1 048	1 600	84.8	52.7
Supplementary VAT (monopoly products)	172[2]	124	176	280	41.9	59.1
Petroleum consumption tax	–	45	54	90	20.0	66.7
Motor vehicles purchase tax	14	21	43	120	104.8	179.1
Banking and insurance tax	59	59	94	130	59.3	38.3
Stamp duty	106	182	249	360	36.8	44.6
Fees	76	100	186	240	86.0	29.0
Taxes on foreign trade	370	746	1 008	1 660	35.1	64.7
Customs duty	148	217	296	470	36.4	58.8
Customs duty on petroleum	14	6	6	10	0.0	66.7
VAT on imports	143[2]	384	530	825	38.0	55.7
Stamp duty imports	18	74	120	250	62.2	108.3
Wharf duty	41	62	54	100	–12.9	85.2
Other	6	3	2	5	–33.3	150.0
Abolished taxes	18	159	20	50	–87.4	150.0
Total tax revenues	2 372	3 829	5 991	8 860	56.5	47.9
Non-tax regular revenues	328	458	637	960	39.1	50.7
Corporate profits and State shares	57	28	33	46	17.9	39.4
Revenues of State property	19	31	69	175	122.6	153.6
Interests and claims	16	38	60	57	55.3	–5.0
Fines	45	74	110	143	48.6	30.0
Other revenues	191	287	365	539	27.2	47.7
Special revenues	77	124	82	135	–33.9	64.6
Annex budget revenues	63	65	141	165	116.9	17.0
Total non-tax revenues	468	647	860	1 260	32.9	46.5
Total consolidated budget revenues	2 840	4 476	6 851	10 120	53.1	47.7

1. With the introduction of value added tax (VAT) in January 1985, the following taxes were abolished: Sales, communications and advertisement tax, production tax, production tax on petroleum and monopoly products.
2. Indirect taxes replaced by VAT in 1985.

Source: Data submitted by the Ministry of Finance and Customs.

Since 1983, the central government deficit has been financed increasingly by short-term Treasury bond issues, which are traded in secondary markets. At the same time net repayments on the foreign debt were made. As a result of the persistently depreciating exchange rate, foreign debt repayments (net) expressed in Turkish lira are rising quickly and are expected to reach TL 600 billion in 1987.

Special funds

The process of fiscal decentralisation away from customary budgets towards extra-budgetary funds continued in 1986. New funds have been created and the existing ones expanded. The most important sources of financing the extra-budgetary funds is their participation in tax revenues and factor incomes, of which they receive a predetermined share. However, own resources and borrowing also play a role. The funds use their resources for transfer payments, investment expenditure and lending to the private sector mainly for housing. In 1986, the share of special funds in total government expenditure reached 7.7 per cent.

Local governments

After having more than doubled in 1985, local governments again doubled their total spending in 1986 according to official estimates. Investment expenditures have contributed particularly heavily to the spending boom, growing faster than average outlays. Fixed investment of local governments rose by about 175 per cent in 1986. Local government revenues, which mainly consist of predetermined shares of central government tax revenues and to a lesser extent of locally administered taxes, also grew rapidly in 1986, albeit more slowly so that the consolidated financial account of local governments turned into deficit in 1986 after a surplus in 1984 and 1985; the deficit was mainly financed by borrowing abroad.

Increased spending by local authorities in the last two years has been causing concern in the central government as it has contributed decisively to the deterioration in the trade balance in 1986. To counter these developments, the central authorities abolished customs duty exemptions for local governments in May 1986. Steps to contain local entities' foreign borrowing were also taken. However, as investment projects in infrastructure often display a certain inertia once they are under way, the deceleration in growth of local government investment and foreign borrowing may be rather moderate in 1987.

State Economic Enterprises

State Economic Enterprises benefited both from the favourable economic environment in the first half of the 1980s and their increasing autonomy under the government's liberalisation programme. Their financial performance, as measured by the surplus of sales revenues over operational expenditures, improved substantially right up to the end of last year. The overall borrowing requirement of SEEs was reduced from 6.6 per cent of GNP in 1980 to an estimated 3.8 per cent of GNP in 1986 (Table 21). Moreover, unlike previous years when they received financial aid from the central government, the SEEs appear to have added positively to the financial account of the central government in 1986.

As a result of the improved financial position of the SEEs, their investment expenditure has increased rapidly in recent years. After a real growth of gross fixed investment of more than 12 per cent in 1985, a decline in volume terms was envisaged for 1986. The strong rise of investment in the course of the first half of the year, however, forced the authorities in May 1986 to make State enterprises subject to the same measures that were applied to local

Table 21. **Financial account of the State Economic Enterprises**

TL billion

	1980	1981	1982	1983	1984	1985	1986[1]
Sales revenues	1 146	1 767	2 650	3 596	6 310	9 319	12 612
Operating expenses	1 169	1 759	2 583	3 630	5 845	8 486	11 387
Operating surplus	–23	8	67	–34	465	833	1 225
Direct taxes	15	41	57	126	117	282	638
Income after taxes	–38	–33	10	–160	348	551	587
Depreciation	23	28	48	155	240	375	545
Subsidies	30	74	76	108	173	248	156
Transfers from budget	149	219	191	278	239	181	138
Cash flow	164	288	325	381	1 000	1 355	1 426
Fixed investment	281	409	533	585	963	1 679	2 426
Changes in stocks	178	210	151	145	545	526	435
External financing requirement	–295	–328	–359	–349	–508	–850	–1 435
Financing:							
Foreign borrowing, net	68	122	104	138	177	466	755
Borrowing	102	180	192	222	520	768	1 215
Repayment	–34	–58	–88	–84	–343	–302	–460
Domestic borrowing, net	227	206	255	211	331	384	680
Central Bank	50	32	31	–5	–56	80	8
State Investment Bank	16	43	59	28	49	19	30
Other domestic borrowing	161	131	165	188	338	285	642

1. Provisional.
Source: State Planning Organisation, *Main Economic Indicators*.

government entities in order to contain spending and avoid overheating of the economy. The 1987 budget programme assumes a continuation of the improvement in the SEEs' financial position and an increase in the positive net financial flow to the Government.

The improved financial status of the SEEs may also lend further stimulus to the implementation of the privatisation programme. The programme has been discussed since 1983 and the legal basis for it was established in 1986 after preparation of a privatisation master plan with the help of foreign consultants. The principal objective of the privatisation programme is to make the economy more responsive to market forces, increase industrial efficiency and promote real growth. It should also help to develop a capital market. As a desirable side effect, the implementation of the programme would generate revenues for the government and minimise financial support for the SEEs by the Treasury. According to this plan most of the existing 35 SEEs and their numerous subsidiaries will be subject to privatisation. However, three categories of SEEs were distinguished which should be sold to the public in three subsequent steps. A first group of four enterprises (a fodder producer, a cement manufacturer, a hotel chain and an airport handling company) could be privatised immediately, which should establish the credibility of the privatisation concept. A second group of SEEs would require some reorganisation before they could be considered for sale. A third group of SEEs could only be privatised in the long run after substantial restructuring.

The Public Participation Fund, which was established in 1984 to finance infrastructure investment and which became operational in 1985, will serve as an intermediary in organising the privatisation programme. The Fund is at present financed mainly through the sale of revenue-sharing certificates as well as through project loans from abroad. So far, progress of the privatisation programme has been slow. Apart from organisational problems, an important concern that may impede the rapid implementation of the programme is the question whether there is enough capital available in the markets to make such a far-reaching economic restructuring feasible. It has frequently been pointed out that gold plays an important role as households' store of value in Turkey, which can be inferred from high imports of gold in the past, and that it should be possible to channel at least a certain proportion of this capital into privatisation. Apart from the question as to whether this requires additional incentives to effect such a shift in private portfolios, it remains to be seen whether the new Istanbul stock exchange would be able to handle effectively a vastly increased volume of business.

III. SHORT-TERM FORECASTS

For 1987, the official growth target for real GNP has been put at 5 per cent. However, given the underlying strength of domestic demand and a carry- over from the second half of 1986, real GNP growth may well exceed the target. Labour incomes are assumed to decelerate, though not faster than inflation. With employment rising further and the savings ratio assumed to decline there should be room for strong growth of real private consumption in 1987 and 1988. Business surveys point to buoyant private investment though its rate of growth may be somewhat lower than in the preceding year. According to policy announcements, the growth of public expenditure will be contained, in particular for investment purposes, in order to reduce the current external deficit. *Inter alia*, and as pointed out above, the exemptions from customs duties granted to local governments have been abolished and other steps were taken

Table 22. **Short-term forecast**

	1985 Current prices TL billion	Percentage volume change over previous year		
		1986	1987	1988
		Provisional	Forecast	
Private consumption	20 181	9.7	5.3	6.0
Public consumption	2 332	8.8	6.0	6.5
Private investment	2 334	13.8	8.0	8.0
Public investment	3 228	13.7	7.5	8.3
Final domestic demand	28 075	10.5	5.8	6.5
Stockbuilding[1]	240	0.4	–0.7	–0.5
Total domestic demand	28 315	10.9	5.1	6.0
Exports of goods and services	6 809	3.4	9.4	6.0
Imports of goods and services	–7 334	16.2	3.2	5.1
Foreign balance[1]	–525	–2.9	1.3	0.2
GNP, market prices	27 789	8.0	6.5	6.2
GNP price deflator		30.6	27.0	25.0
Consumption price deflator		34.0	30.0	27.0
		$ million		
Balance of payments				
Exports (fob)	8 255	7 583	8 200	8 700
Imports (fob)	11 230	10 664	11 600	11 900
Trade balance	–2 975	–3 081	–3 400	–3 200
Invisibles	1 962	1 553	1 700	1 800
Current balance	–1 013	–1 528	–1 700	–1 400

1. Contribution to GNP growth.
Sources: State Planning Organisation, *Main Economic Indicators;* OECD Secretariat estimates.

in 1986 to constrain local entities' as well as State Economic Enterprises' investment spending. However, due to the strength of investment in 1986 and the multi-year dimension of most infrastructure investments, growth of public investment is predicted to be well above the growth of GNP. Hence public spending will continue to exert an expansionary impact on the economy in 1987 and 1988, although somewhat less than in 1986 (Table 22).

Monetary policy is assumed to be somewhat more restrictive in 1987 and beyond with reduced growth of monetary aggregates, to achieve further disinflation. Given the forecast price deceleration and easing of demand pressures, this may allow short-term interest rates to remain roughly constant and long-term rates to decline over the forecast period. As the damping effects of imported oil and other raw material prices are expected to disappear, underlying domestic price increases as well as the continued depreciation of the effective exchange rate of the lira may make it difficult to reduce inflation. Much will also depend on the harvest in 1987/88.

With the growth of activity decelerating but remaining strong, employment is predicted to grow at a lower rate than last year. Due to the problems of gauging hidden unemployment and forecasting its evolution, the growth of the labour force is difficult to foresee. This forecast assumes an increase below that of employment, which would result in a further decline in the unemployment ratio.

Forecasting the foreign balance is particularly uncertain this time. Import growth is expected to decelerate in line with the slowdown of domestic demand expansion. However, there may be an upward risk on imports as domestic demand will remain relatively strong. On the export side, the predicted pick-up in 1987/88 assumes market share gains similar to those of the first half of the 1980s as a result of the adopted exchange rate and export promotion policy. However, relevant export markets are expected to shrink this year and to recover only moderately thereafter, which requires a comparatively strong offsetting competitiveness effect and unhampered access to foreign markets; there is thus a downside risk embodied in the present export forecast. Given the likelihood of somewhat deteriorating terms of trade, the deficit in the current account of the balance of payments is not expected to improve and could possibly worsen in 1987 and 1988.

IV. STRUCTURAL ADJUSTMENT IN THE PUBLIC SECTOR

General government revenues and expenditures as a share of GNP have remained relatively low. Thus, although government expenditures rose to a peak of 28.5 per cent of GNP when expansionary policies were followed during the 1970s, they have since fallen to around 25 per cent of GNP (Table 23). Preliminary estimates for 1986 point to another increase to about 27.3 per cent. This contrasts markedly with developments in other OECD countries where general government expenditures have risen sharply over the last two decades, absorbing by now close to half of domestic resources. Similarly, the budget deficit has fluctuated in a relatively narrow band between one and two per cent of GNP in recent years, with the exception of 1984, when it accelerated to almost 4 per cent of GNP, mainly as the result of a slowdown in the growth of revenues. If the financing needs – mainly for investment purposes – of the large State sector composed of public utilities, banks and industrial and commercial enterprises, are taken into account, the State's borrowing requirement on a cash basis has been considerably higher, i.e. 5 to 6 per cent of GNP (Table 18).

In spite of the comparatively favourable situation of the general government accounts, there have been problems because of poor management and inadequate administrative structures in the public sector which, for many years, called for reform: tax evasion and avoidance were widespread, especially among the self-employed, whilst the income tax burden for fixed-income earners of moderate means tended to increase substantially due to fiscal drag. In addition, the penalty system for tax delinquents was inadequate. Excessive centralisation, coupled with a proliferation of administrative checks, led to delays in decision-making and to uneconomic choices of priorities. Municipalities had insufficient funds for providing essential public services, and the public enterprise sector had become a burden on the State because of low productivity and financial losses.

Whilst reforms to deal with these issues had been discussed by Parliament for many years, an effective programme was only initiated in 1980 and reinforced in late 1983, following general elections. The measures dealing with tax reform will be discussed in more detail below. The programme also included streamlining of the administration, the reduction of the role of the State in the economy, and increased decentralisation through the creation of special investment agencies and through greater financial independence of local administrations. Another important decision was the privatisation of the so-called «productive» State enterprises, after various attempts in the last ten years to improve their management and financial performance through administrative reorganisation and government exhortations seemed to have failed. There was surprisingly little opposition to selling the SEEs to the public – even though about one-third of the industrial labour force is employed by this sector. Whilst parliamentary procedures for carrying through this undertaking have been completed, organisational and technical problems have so far prevented the programme from getting off the ground.

Table 23. **General government consolidated account**

As per cent of GNP

	1965	1970	1975	1980	1981	1982	1983	1984	1985
Revenues	19.1	24.4	25.7	25.1	26.5	24.8	25.8	21.2	23.2
Tax revenues	14.8	17.2	18.3	17.8	19.0	18.2	17.7	14.6	16.4
Central government	13.4	15.7	17.7	16.9	18.2	17.4	16.7	12.9	13.8
Local administration	1.4	1.5	0.6	0.9	0.8	0.8	1.0	1.3	1.6
Special funds	–	–	–	–	–	–	–	0.4	1.0
Social security premiums	1.4	3.0	4.3	3.2	3.2	3.3	3.4	3.0	2.9
Non-tax revenues	2.9	4.2	3.1	4.1	4.3	3.3	4.7	3.6	3.9
Central government	1.7	3.3	2.4	3.7	3.2	2.0	3.3	2.4	2.3
Local administration	1.2	0.4	0.4	0.0	0.7	0.7	0.8	0.5	0.7
Social security institutions	0.0	0.5	0.3	0.4	0.4	0.6	0.6	0.7	0.5
Special funds	–	–	–	–	–	–	–	–	0.4
Expenditures	21.1	25.0	24.6	28.5	27.3	26.4	27.7	25.0	24.7
Current expenditures	11.1	11.6	11.6	11.8	10.2	10.3	10.2	9.0	8.5
(Personnel)	(3.0)	(3.7)	(6.0)	(8.8)	(6.8)	(7.3)	(6.4)	(5.6)	(5.2)
Central government	10.0	10.0	10.5	10.5	9.2	9.4	9.2	8.1	7.5
Local administration	1.1	1.3	0.9	1.1	0.9	0.8	0.9	0.8	0.9
Social security institutions	0.0	0.3	0.2	0.2	0.1	0.1	0.1	0.1	0.1
Special funds	–	–	–	–	–	–	–	–	–
Investment expenditures	5.4	5.4	5.2	5.8	6.3	6.1	5.1	4.5	5.3
Central government	4.6	4.8	4.7	5.0	5.6	5.3	4.2	3.7	3.6
Local administration	0.8	0.6	0.5	0.8	0.7	0.8	0.9	0.8	1.1
Social security institutions	0.0	0.0	0.0	0.0	0.0	0.0	0.0	0.0	0.0
Special funds	–	–	–	–	–	–	–	0.0	0.6
Transfer expenditures	4.6	8.0	7.8	10.9	10.8	10.0	12.4	11.5	10.9
Central government	3.9	4.8	4.9	7.8	7.5	6.5	8.3	7.8	7.1
Local administration	0.4	0.5	0.2	0.1	0.1	0.1	0.2	0.2	0.3
Social security institutions	0.3	2.7	2.7	3.0	3.2	3.4	3.9	3.5	3.4
Special funds	–	–	–	–	–	–	–	0.0	0.1
Balance	–2.0	–0.6	1.1	–3.4	–0.8	–1.6	–1.9	–3.8	–1.5

Source: OECD Secretariat calculations based on data submitted by the Turkish authorities.

The following sections will discuss in more detail the structure of general government expenditure and revenues as well as specific aspects of the reforms introduced over the last five years. The concluding paragraphs will address the issue of the public debt and problems arising from increasing debt service payments.

General government accounts

The data presented below and in the Statistical Annex represent an attempt by the Secretariat to bring together for the first time on a coherent basis statistics of various public sector entities. As detailed public sector accounts on a national income basis are not as yet compiled in Turkey, an international comparison of the data is difficult. However, apart from questions relating to methods and definitions, the data are considered to be complete and should provide an overview of the general government sector.

Expenditures: A significant feature of the structure of general government expenditure is the relatively low share of social security expenditures (and revenues) in total government spending. It is currently not quite 15 per cent, whilst its share of nominal GNP is below 4 per

Table 24. **General government accounts**

	1965	1970	1975	1980	1981	1982	1983	1984	1985
Revenues per cent of total									
Central government	79.5	77.7	78.2	82.0	80.5	78.5	77.5	72.1	69.8
Local administrations	13.0	7.5	3.8	4.0	5.9	6.0	6.8	8.0	10.1
Social security institutions	7.5	14.8	18.0	14.0	13.6	15.5	15.7	18.0	14.6
Special funds	–	–	–	–	–	–	–	1.9	5.5
Per cent of GNP	19.1	24.4	25.7	25.1	26.5	24.8	25.8	21.2	23.2
Central government	15.1	19.0	20.1	20.6	21.4	19.4	20.0	15.3	16.1
Local administrations	2.6	1.8	1.0	1.0	1.5	1.5	1.8	1.8	2.3
Social security institutions	1.4	3.6	4.6	3.5	3.6	3.9	4.0	3.7	3.4
Special funds	–	–	–	–	–	–	–	0.4	1.4
Expenditures per cent of total									
Central government	87.6	78.5	81.9	81.3	81.5	80.2	78.0	78.7	73.5
Local administrations	11.1	9.5	6.5	7.2	6.2	6.1	7.3	6.9	9.0
Social security institutions	1.3	12.0	11.6	11.5	12.3	13.7	14.7	14.4	14.3
Special funds	–	–	–	–	–	–	–	–	3.2
Per cent of GNP	21.1	25.0	24.6	28.5	27.3	26.4	27.7	25.0	24.7
Central government	18.5	19.6	20.1	23.3	22.3	21.2	21.7	19.6	18.2
Local administrations	2.3	2.4	1.6	2.0	1.7	1.6	2.0	1.8	2.3
Social security institutions	0.3	3.0	2.9	3.2	3.3	3.6	4.0	3.6	3.5
Special funds	–	–	–	–	–	–	–	0.0	0.7

Source: OECD Secretariat calculations based on data submitted by the Turkish autorities.

cent (Table 24). The social security data are not directly comparable with the data of other countries as some of the expenditures for health services are borne by central government (½ per cent of GNP). The social security organisations insure only a part of the labour force, such as civil servants and workers in industry and services; including dependants, they insure about 27 million people, i.e. about half of the total population. A modernisation of the system is envisaged, giving greater social protection to a larger share of the population but financing problems have so far prevented any headway being made.

The weight of regional authorities in expenditures and revenues has also been rather light in the past and, although the share has recently been increasing, it was just 9 per cent of expenditures in 1985. Nevertheless, closer examination of budget developments from 1980 – when fiscal reforms were first introduced – to 1983, and in the following two years to the end of 1985, reveals that the central government's share of the public budget has fallen and that of local administrations has increased by approximately 50 per cent since 1984 as the consequence of the central authorities' aim to grant greater financial autonomy to local governments, and to increase the share in tax collection which the local authorities are permitted to retain. The data also reveal the growing importance of special investment agencies, the so-called Funds, which were created to improve planning and implementation of the government's social housing and infrastructure investment programme. Their share of expenditures amounted to 3.2 per cent in 1985. The Funds are financed through levies and other indirect taxes, as well as by selling financial participations to the public. Preliminary budget data for 1986 suggest that the public investment decentralisation programme has gathered momentum; expenditure in nominal terms by the special funds rose by around 300 per cent in 1986 (Table 25), which appears to put their current share of general government spending at more than 7 per cent. This, together with the reported rise in expenditures of local authorities in 1986, seems to point to a significant increase in the share of

Table 25. **Consolidated account of special funds**

TL billion

	1984	1985	1986[1]
Revenues	75.1	376.5	1 175.3
Tax revenues	–	276.7	829.3
Direct taxes	–	–	79.3
Indirect taxes	75.1	276.7	750.0
Non-tax revenues	0.1	99.8	346.0
Expenditures	3.7	215.6	986.8
Current expenditures	0.0	8.8	21.6
Investment expenditures	3.4	167.6	480.3
Transfers	0.3	39.2	484.9
Balance	71.4	160.9	188.5
Borrowing	10.0	140.0	311.1
Foreign	–	–	86.1
Domestic	10.0	140.0	225.0
Lending (net)	–51.7	–240.1	–308.9
Private	–51.7	–231.3	–297.9
Government	–	–8.8	–11.0
Change in cash-bank	–29.7	–60.8	–190.7

1. Provisional.
Source: OECD Secretariat calculations based on data submitted by the Turkish authorities.

public sector spending over which the central authorities have in principal given up direct control; its current dimension may be put at close to one-fifth of general government expenditure.

An examination of expenditures by major spending programmes (Table 26) reveals several additional features which may differ from the situation in other countries. A large share of total expenditure – customarily 20 to 25 per cent – is earmarked for operational agencies with an important investment budget such as the Highway Department, the Water Agency, Village and Forest Development, etc. This is, of course, necessary in a country of Turkey's size and geographical configuration, whose infrastructure is still relatively underdeveloped. Considering the harsh climate in Central Anatolia, extensive repairs to transport and communication systems will probably always be an important expenditure item. However, this contrasts markedly with expenditures on education, which have declined from 17 per cent of general government outlay in 1975 to 10 per cent in 1985 (2½ per cent of GNP). Literacy levels in Turkey are still very low; according to the 1985 census, about one-fifth of the population aged over six declared itself illiterate. Although primary school attendance is compulsory for children aged from six to twelve, the quality of primary education varies substantially between regions. Secondary school attendance drops rapidly after the age of 14 to around 30 per cent, and only some 10 per cent of the young continue to pursue university education. Although this is not the place to discuss the issue, it is clear – as in the case of social security coverage – that Turkey has a great deal of ground to cover to reach the standards of education, health care, etc., to which other OECD countries have been accustomed for a long time. Moreover, investment in education and vocational training becomes the more urgent, given the country's aspirations to rapid economic development and the necessity of winning export market shares to finance the development drive.

Table 26. **General government expenditures by spending categories**[1]

	1965	1970	1975	1980	1981	1982	1983	1984	1985
TL billion									
General services	4.6	10.9	30.6	443	616	734	1 116	1 555	1 840
Defence	3.7	5.7	28.8	209	251	324	404	580	833
Other public services	4.0	8.6	27.2	239	386	502	585	833	1 770
Health	0.7	1.2	5.0	49	51	67	85	123	174
Education	2.5	5.3	22.8	159	205	285	352	490	674
Interest payments	0.4	1.0	3.2	28	67	93	181	375	595
Social security outlays	0.2	4.0	14.2	137	210	302	453	631	947
Total expenditures	16.1	36.7	131.8	1 264	1 786	2 307	3 176	4 587	6 833
As per cent of total									
General services	28.6	29.7	23.3	35.0	34.5	31.8	35.1	33.8	26.9
Defence	23.2	15.5	21.8	16.6	14.0	14.0	12.7	12.6	12.2
Other public services	24.8	23.4	20.6	18.9	21.6	21.8	18.4	18.2	25.9
Health	4.3	3.3	3.8	3.9	2.8	2.9	2.7	2.7	2.5
Education	15.5	14.4	17.3	12.6	11.5	12.4	11.1	10.7	9.9
Interest payments	2.4	2.8	2.4	2.2	3.9	4.0	5.7	8.2	8.7
Social security outlays	1.2	10.9	10.8	10.8	11.7	13.1	14.3	13.8	13.9
As per cent of GNP									
General services	6.0	7.5	5.6	10.0	9.5	8.4	9.7	8.5	6.7
Defence	4.7	3.9	5.4	4.7	3.8	3.7	3.5	3.2	3.0
Other public services	5.2	5.8	5.1	5.4	5.9	5.7	5.1	4.5	6.5
Health	1.0	0.8	0.9	1.1	0.8	0.8	0.7	0.7	0.6
Education	3.4	3.6	4.3	3.5	3.1	3.3	3.0	2.6	2.4
Interest payments	0.5	0.7	0.6	0.6	1.0	1.1	1.6	2.0	2.1
Social security outlays	0.3	2.7	2.7	3.0	3.2	3.4	3.9	3.5	3.4
Total expenditures	21.1	25.0	24.6	28.5	27.3	26.4	27.7	25.0	24.7

1. Spending categories correspond to the normal budget presentation:
General services: All administrative departments;
Defence: Ministry of Defence, armed services and gendarmerie;
Other public services: Investment agencies (i.e. Highways Department, water development agency etc.);
Health: Ministry of Health and university hospitals;
Education: Ministry of Education and university administrations.

Source: OECD Secretariat calculations based on data submitted by the Turkish authorities.

The breakdown of budget expenditures by broad functions into current expenditures, investment outlay and transfer payments shows that an effort has been made from 1980 onwards to contain the growth of expenditures on purchases of current services and public investment. Notably, employment in public services was reduced through not filling vacancies and limitation of creation of new posts. As a result of this, as well as restraint in granting wage increases, personnel expenditures fell from 8.8 per cent to 5.2 per cent of GNP in 1985. Central government investment outlay as a share of GNP also fell as spending programmes were streamlined and priorities were reassessed. However, this was partly compensated by increased investments of local administrations and more recently of the investment funds.

Transfer payments remained at around 10 to 11 per cent of GNP because the reduction of subsidies and other transfers to State enterprises was balanced by an increase in new subsidies to low income earners and to exporters (tax rebates), as well as by rising interest payments.

An indirect indication of the resources restraint which the Turkish authorities are facing in modernising their society, and the economy specifically, is the sharp increase in interest payments on the public debt. Interest payments have risen from around 2 per cent of expenditures in the 1970s to currently 10 per cent; in fact, they now absorb as great a share of the economy's resources as expenditures on education. The recent increase in the interest burden is the result of two factors: first, the sharp rise in the central government budget deficit to 4 per cent of GNP in 1984, and second, the accompanying decision to resort to market financing of the deficit through issuing short-term Treasury bills at competitive interest rates. In order to make the system attractive to investors, interest rates were set somewhat above market rates; at present, Treasury bills and bonds are sold by public tender. Last but not least, interest payments on the foreign debt rise as the result of a gradual real devaluation of the lira.

Revenues: The equally low share of tax revenues in GNP has already been stressed (Table 23). As the following statistic shows, it is also low in international comparison (Table 27). Including social security contributions, it has averaged some 20 per cent of GNP in Turkey over the last 15 years whilst in several other OECD Member countries this ratio has risen over a comparable period to between 28 and 45 per cent of GNP; the OECD average of the share of government revenues in GNP is currently about 37 per cent. These figures are, however, a rather inadequate measure of the tax pressure on individual taxpayers. The absolute size of GNP expressed in a common currency, the size of the non-imposable population and the degree of tax evasion also play a role. There thus seems to be a certain logic that countries with a relatively low GNP per capita, high population growth and a less modern fiscal system also appear to have a lower share of taxes in GNP. Turkey, however, is not only – as one might have inferred – at the bottom of the league in this regard; the lag in terms of percentage shares *vis-à-vis* all other countries has also widened.

Diagram 10. **Major components of tax revenues**

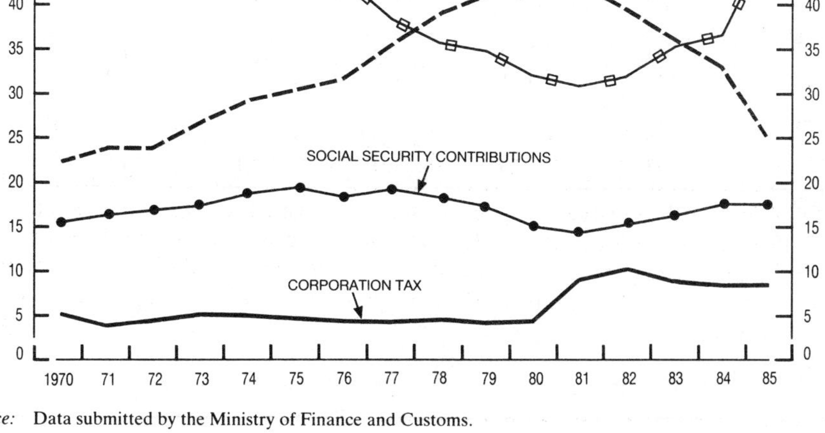

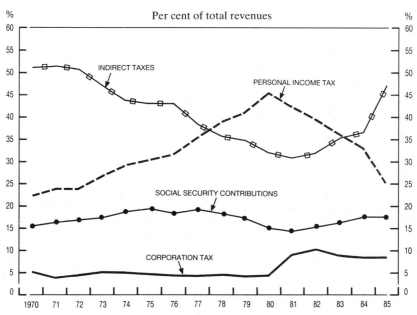

Source: Data submitted by the Ministry of Finance and Customs.

Table 27. **Relative shares of tax revenues**

	Percentage share of total					Total tax revenue as per cent of GDP
	Personal income	Corporate	Goods and services	Property	Social security contribution	
Turkey						
1965	21.1	6.5	61.8	1.6	8.9	16.5
1970	22.1	5.1	51.0	6.4	15.4	20.3
1975	30.3	4.6	43.0	2.7	19.4	22.7
1980	45.3	4.3	31.9	3.6	14.9	20.9
1984	32.9	8.4	37.1	4.2	17.4	17.7
1985	24.7	8.4	46.9	4.9	15.1	19.3
Greece						
1970	10.1	1.7	50.2	9.6	27.1	24.3
1984	14.5	2.5	43.0	2.6	34.8	35.2
Ireland						
1970	18.3	8.8	52.4	12.2	8.2	31.2
1984	30.7	3.3	45.1	3.8	14.6	39.5
Finland						
1970	41.8	5.5	40.8	2.3	4.8	31.6
1984	45.7	4.4	38.0	2.8	8.7	36.0
Portugal						
1970	..	..	44.6	4.2	23.9	34.1
1984	..	..	43.9	1.8	25.9	32.0
Spain						
1970	11.5	8.2	35.9	6.5	37.4	17.2
1984	22.7	5.0	25.5	3.8	41.1	28.4
Germany						
1970	26.7	5.7	31.8	4.9	30.3	32.9
1984	27.9	5.4	27.1	3.3	36.4	37.7
France						
1970	11.8	6.3	37.3	3.6	36.2	35.6
1984	13.3	4.1	28.7	4.4	43.6	45.5
Italy						
1970	10.9	6.6	38.7	6.0	37.8	27.9
1984	26.3	9.8	26.1	2.9	33.9	41.2
United Kingdom						
1970	31.1	9.3	28.8	12.4	13.9	37.2
1984	26.7	11.5	30.5	12.3	18.2	38.3
OECD total						
1970	28.2	9.0	34.8	7.1	19.8	30.0
1984	31.8	7.9	30.0	5.1	24.0	37.1

Source: OECD, *Revenue Statistics.*

A characteristic of the fiscal system has been that incomes in agriculture have, until recently, remained largely untaxed. In addition, many of the self-employed were able to understate their incomes for tax assessment purposes. The share of indirect taxes in total revenues has therefore traditionally been relatively high (some 50 per cent during the 1960s and early 1970s). However, this share fell from the mid-1970s to the beginning of the 1980s for a variety of reasons, i.e. financial difficulties of several State enterprises, which failed to pass on indirect taxes collected, negative growth of GNP in 1979 and 1980, and the granting of tax concessions on imports in order to stimulate exports (Diagram 10).

By contrast, the share of personal income tax, which had been only one-fifth of government revenues at the beginning of the 1970s, rose to over 45 per cent in 1980 as the consequence of inflation on unchanged tax rates and brackets. Corporation tax in relative terms, however, did not increase at all until 1980 since many enterprises, and in particular the SEEs, posted losses or were exempt from tax because of generous investment allowances.

Fiscal reform programme

Work on a major fiscal reform was started in 1980 following introduction of the new stabilization and structural adjustment programme in January. Its far-reaching and quasi-revolutionary character in the Turkish context appears to have gone largely unnoticed; but without it, the improvements in economic performance and the success achieved so far in reducing inflation would probably not have been possible. One major reason that the tax reform has been a relative success may be that it has been introduced gradually over a span of five years, yet its principal aims have been to correct the injustice that only relatively few – mainly fixed-income earners and large corporations – were regular contributors to government direct revenue receipts and to increase the flow of regular revenues to the government budget.

Starting from 1981, efforts were intensified to audit more regularly the self-employed and owners of small businesses; lump sum tax limits were adjusted and minimum tax increased in line with inflation. Farmers were made liable to income tax, and absentee landowners lost the tax exemptions granted to farmers. Withholding tax rates were increased on income from bonds, shares and bank deposits, and unregistered property sales were made subject to tax. Furthermore, taxes on real estate were increased substantially. Litigation procedures were modernised in order to prevent tax avoidance through lengthy legal action. Last but not least, the introduction of a general value-added tax was announced to replace the old system of excise and stamp duties on a limited number of transactions or commodities. Withholding tax on financial assets and interest income, and several indirect taxes, were lowered in the following years, whilst additional levies were introduced in order to provide a source of income for the various funds.

For the majority of fixed-income earners, the principal news was no doubt the announced adjustment of tax rates and brackets which promised relief from high income tax that in many instances took away close to half of earned income, even for tax-payers of relatively modest means. The basic personal income tax rate was set at 40 per cent for incomes up to TL 1 million, but there was a relatively high tax-free minimum income. The base rate was to be successively lowered to 25 per cent by 1985, with the highest marginal tax rate falling from 75 per cent to 50 per cent of imposable income.

The new Government elected in November 1983 provided some additional tax relief for fixed-income earners through a system of tax rebates against receipts for purchases of essential services and food. The receipts were used as checks on the liberal professions and on sales points to detect undeclared income. It is difficult to assess whether the system has been efficient. After the tax reform was introduced in 1981, the elasticity of direct and indirect taxes improved substantially (Table 28). But the elasticity fell thereafter, indicating that the new controls may not have been very effective. However, the latter period also coincided with the so-called "broker crisis" during which a considerable number of enterprises and commercial banks experienced serious liquidity problems or encountered losses, and revenue losses to the Treasury were substantial. The year 1984 was exceptional in the sense that the Government allowed substantial tax relief and lowered a number of indirect taxes in order to stimulate exports and investments. But the data for 1985 show that with the introduction of value-added tax the elasticity of both direct and indirect taxes increased considerably. The tax reform thus seems to have achieved its principal aim of stopping or possibly reversing the erosion of real after-tax incomes of wage-earners and pensioners, whilst somewhat improving the tax base. Much will probably depend in future on the efficiency of the tax administration in making use of the new control instruments to upgrade tax collection efficiency and broaden the tax base permanently. As could be seen from the discussion of the composition of public expenditure, an increase in the share of revenues in GNP from its present relatively low level would be desirable in order to improve the authorities' possibilities for providing a larger volume of public services, including better standards of social care and education.

Table 28. **Tax elasticities**

	Tax revenues				Social security contribution
	Total	Total direct taxes	Personal income tax	Indirect taxes	
1975	1.67	1.72	1.98	1.67	1.95
1976	1.37	1.47	1.48	1.25	0.98
1977	1.08	1.57	1.66	0.64	1.33
1978	0.97	1.19	1.24	0.72	0.80
1979	0.92	0.98	1.02	0.85	0.77
1980	0.85	0.99	0.99	0.65	0.55
1981	1.22	1.29	0.95	1.07	1.05
1982	0.84	0.74	0.61	1.02	1.17
1983	0.89	0.61	0.61	1.35	1.15
1984	0.52	0.43	0.37	0.64	0.74
1985[1]	1.37	0.71	0.47	2.20	0.82

1. In 1985 the value added tax was introduced.
Source: OECD Secretariat calculations based on data submitted by the Turkish authorities.

Government debt

Over the years, continuous general budget deficits have led to an increase of the public medium- and long-term debt (domestic and foreign) to 45 per cent of GNP by 1985. The rise was particularly marked in the last five to six years, when borrowing abroad was substantial and continuous devaluation of the lira increased the value of the debt expressed in domestic currency. Switching over to market financing of the budget deficit also increased the interest burden. As mentioned in the preceding section, interest payments currently absorb about 10 per cent of general government expenditure; the yield to investors on Treasury bonds is somewhat higher than the rates of return on other financial investments, particularly for time deposits and private bond issues; the rate was 60 per cent (net of tax) in 1984 and around 50 per cent in 1986 (Table 29).

Table 29. **Indicators of the public debt burden**

	1980	1981	1982	1983	1984	1985	1986
Public debt (TL billion)	1 155	1 876	2 920	4 810	8 205	12 550	20 011[1]
Public debt (per cent of GNP)	26.0	28.6	33.5	41.6	44.6	45.6	51.1
Non-interest budget balance (TL billion)	–121	18	–50	–7	–255	169	193
Growth of nominal GNP (per cent)	101.6	47.8	33.2	32.2	59.1	50.8	41.1
Treasury bond interest (per cent)	–	–	–	45.0	59.0	56.0	50.0

1. Preliminary estimates.
Source: OECD Secretariat calculations based on data submitted by the Turkish authorities.

Currently, interest rates on new government bond issues exceed the rate of growth of nominal GNP, but the "implied" interest rate calculated on the total stock of debt is still considerably lower – probably around 30 per cent – due to the fact that the longer-term government debt incurred before 1984 carries considerably lower nominal rates. An increase in the average interest rate on the public debt would tend to widen the government deficit and thus stimulate the mechanism by which higher deficits feed into higher public debt which, through higher interest payments, result in still higher deficits. Even if present levels of government deficits and nominal GNP growth would appear consistent with public debt falling as a share of GNP, the potential increase in the average interest rate on the public debt could imply a risk of interest payments "crowding out" other items on the government budget or leading to higher taxes, as the authorities would attempt to prevent deficits getting too large. This, evidently, would reduce the possibilities for improving essential public services and have a compressing effect on the public investment programme and hence on future economic growth prospects. There may also be a risk that a rapidly rising public debt would affect inflationary expectations unfavourably, as it could create fears that future governments might attempt to solve the domestic debt problem through the monetisation of public debt, as was the case in the past.

Whilst the general government deficits of the last two years have been a relatively stable and low proportion of GNP (around 2 per cent) and the non-interest budget balance was in surplus, it would be advisable to take precautions to forestall future increases of deficits by continuing efforts to eliminate inefficiencies and to control carefully the expansion of public spending programmes. Especially, it appears that the rapid growth of expenditure by special funds and local governments may not be sustainable and needs to be checked, also for balance-of-payments considerations. There may, furthermore, be more scope for increasing government revenues through strengthening activities directed at reducing tax evasion and broadening the tax base.

V. CONCLUSIONS

In 1986, real GNP growth at around 8 per cent was the highest experienced by OECD Member countries. The acceleration of activity was particularly marked in agriculture and manufacturing industry, and appears to have led to capacity bottlenecks in specific sectors. The vigorous expansion was due entirely to strong growth of domestic demand, both of consumption and investment, whilst the contribution of the real foreign balance to growth became negative.

Contrary to what might be expected under conditions of high capacity utilisation, inflation decelerated further, though at around 30 per cent it remained at a high level. The deceleration of the price rise was helped – as in other countries – by the fall in oil and other commodity prices and the weakening of the US dollar; moderating monetary expansion, decelerating growth of unit labour cost, and a good harvest also contributed to containing price rises.

The fall of the oil price led to savings on the import bill by about $1.5 billion. However, Middle East oil exporters reduced their imports from Turkey by approximately $1 billion and receipts from invisible transactions such as net tourism earnings and workers' remittances also decreased moderately. The net benefit from the oil price fall was thus not very significant; moreover, accelerating domestic demand led to higher imports. As a result, the external deficit rose to $1.5 billion. Whilst the higher deficit could be financed by increased foreign official and private borrowing, the fact that it rose significantly should be taken as a reminder that the current external deficit tends to worsen when domestic demand rises relative to export demand. The continuation of growth rates of domestic demand as high as in 1986 would not appear to be sustainable on either domestic or balance-of-payments grounds, given that the country's foreign exchange reserves are not very high, and amortisation payments on the foreign debt absorb a substantial share of export earnings. The improvement registered in Turkey's international credit-worthiness over the last four to five years may be reversed, should the current account deficit tend to rise rather than fall due to the relative weakening of export growth.

For 1987, the official growth target has been put at 5 per cent but, due to carry-over effects from 1986 and the dynamic state of domestic demand, GNP growth could well be more than one percentage point higher. Private consumption may gradually lose momentum but is still likely to grow by some 5 per cent. Business surveys point to further strengthening of private investment, and public investment is likely to be boosted by the continuation of large infrastructure investments which were started in recent years. With the contribution of the real foreign balance to GNP growth also turning positive, the deceleration in activity in 1987 is likely to be only moderate. However, given the likelihood of some deterioration in the terms of trade, the deficit in the current account of the balance of payments is not expected to improve and could possibly worsen.

Analysis of Turkish export performance over the past ten years reveals both structural weaknesses and encouraging aspects. On the one hand, external competitiveness has improved considerably since a policy of gradual real depreciation of the exchange rate was adopted; unit labour costs in a common currency have apparently risen less than abroad. Most of Turkey's positive export performance in the first half of the 1980s can be explained by this effect. On the other hand, there is still a need to improve the product structure of Turkish merchandise exports through greater diversification of production and a shift from unprocessed goods to merchandise with a higher share of value added. Because the switch from domestic to exports markets entails extra cost for entrepreneurs, temporary fiscal advantages had been granted to Turkish exporters; when these were reduced from 1984, export growth slowed down. The strong decline of industrial exports in 1986 prompted the authorities to reintroduce tax rebates for export sales to a certain extent. It should be recognised that over the medium term such measures cannot replace a coherent adjustment strategy built principally on sound demand management policy and management of the exchange rate, as well as recognised forms of export promotion through official export credit insurance, and government trade promotion offices.

An important causal factor of the surge in imports of investment goods in 1986 has been the greater financial autonomy given to local authorities and to extra-budgetary investment funds. Decentralisation of public investment activity was introduced in order to improve resource allocation and achieve gains in overall economic efficiency. But the 1986 episode, when local governments and special funds used their newly-acquired spending authority to an extent not anticipated by the central government, has exposed the risks that are attached to an easing of central control. The Turkish authorities have apparently introduced adequate measures to check from now on the acceleration of investment activities of State enterprises and of local administrations, notably insofar as imports and foreign borrowing are concerned. But it may be more difficult to control growth of the overall level of public investment, given the fact that ongoing projects normally cannot be stopped and often entail additional and possibly continuous expenditure once realised. Another worrying feature is that investment by the manufacturing sector is still relatively weak, given capacity constraints and the need to expand exports. It cannot be excluded that this weakness may be due to some extent to the crowding-out effect of continuous government borrowing. There is thus a need to be more selective in planning public sector investments and to ensure that the public sector borrowing requirement is reduced.

Substantial progress has been made in recent years in respect of making monetary instruments more effective and creating better functioning capital markets. The Central Bank has strengthened supervision of commercial banks, introduced a unified required reserve ratio, opened an inter-bank market for short-term maturities and overnight funds, and established a secondary market for government securities through which it can conduct open-market operations to regulate bank liquidity. There are advanced plans to encourage enterprises to go public and to increase the flow of tradeable paper in the recently opened stock exchange in Istanbul.

Another area in which structural reform appears to have been relatively successful is monetary targeting. This is a particularly difficult task in a country with a large agricultural sector, and highly seasonal money demand and income flows. The Central Bank has chosen M2 as the principal indicator. The question may be asked, however, if another monetary aggregate, i.e. M2X, should not be considered for this purpose, as foreign exchange deposits represent a substantial part of banks' liabilities, and there is evidence of an increasing volume of domestic transactions carried out in foreign exchange.

The adjustment policies introduced since 1980 in the areas of public administration and government finances are commencing to show positive results. Revenue collection, which was plagued for many years by widespread tax evasion and accumulation of payment arrears has improved, whilst reform of income tax scales has led to an easing of the direct tax burden on the average tax-payer. This seems to have been helped significantly by the introduction of value-added tax, and the policy of granting tax rebates for purchases of life's essentials, both of which have increased the capacity of the tax administration to check tax returns for possible fraud. The creation of separate public investment agencies, the so-called special funds, which are financed by levies earmarked for this purpose and by the sale of revenue participation shares, has apparently improved the efficiency of public investment programmes for infrastructure projects and has started to alleviate the shortage of low-cost housing. The general government deficit has been kept stable at around 2 per cent of GNP in the last two years and has been financed increasingly through the sale of short-term Treasury bonds at market rates of interest. Monetisation of government debt has thus been considerably reduced, which had a damping effect on domestic inflation. However, given the buoyancy of investments by special funds and municipalities noted earlier, and the present low absolute level of government consumption and social transfers, care needs to be taken to monitor and control the development of the public sector borrowing requirement with the aim of preventing deficits from widening.

On balance, current developments of the macroeconomic aggregates reveal that stabilization and adjustment policies followed in recent years have broadly had the desired results; whilst inroads have been made on inflation (though its overall level is still high) growth of GNP and employment have been comparatively buoyant. International competitiveness has improved, thanks mainly to a policy of gradual real devaluation of the lira, helped by temporary fiscal incentives. However, the deterioration of the current balance in 1986 should be considered as a timely warning that an excessive acceleration of domestic demand always carries the risk of compromising the gains in performance achieved earlier. Particular care also needs to be taken to prevent general government deficits from rising above recent average levels, as had apparently happened in 1986; higher government deficits tend to worsen the current account balance and, by crowding out private productive capital formation, would weaken medium-term growth prospects.

NOTES

1. See E.E. Leamer and R.M. Stern, (1970): *Quantitative International Economics,* Boston, and Annex II of this Survey.
2. Germany, Iran, Iraq, the United Kingdom, the United States, Saudi Arabia, Italy, France, the Netherlands, Switzerland, Belgium-Luxembourg, other OECD, Comecon, Libya, other OPEC, and the rest of the world.
3. A student test shows that the t-ratio is –3.1, i.e. the calculated coefficient of determination is significant at a 99 per cent level of confidence.

Annex I

NOMINAL WAGES, INFLATION AND THE NAIRU

The Phillips curve represents a dynamic adjustment process of nominal wages to equilibrium (steady state) and disequilibrium phenomena. A general formulation of the short-run Phillips curve, applicable to a variety of institutional arrangements, relates the rate of change of the wage rate (WR) to a measure of past or expected consumer price inflation, the unemployment rate and a vector of other possibly relevant variables. The main equilibrium characteristics of the wage formation process are the expected rate of inflation and trend productivity growth, the latter covered by the constant of the Phillips equation. The disequilibrium component of the equation is represented by the unemployment rate, which approximates excess of supply in the labour market.

Numerous specifications were tested by the OECD Secretariat for the Turkish Phillips curve, including, for example, actual productivity growth, terms-of-trade proxies and allowing for hysteresis[1]. Given the simultaneous determination of wages and prices, all equations were estimated by simultaneous estimation techniques on seasonally-adjusted semi-annual data. The estimation period runs from the first half of 1974 to the second half of 1985. Percentage changes refer to semi-annual changes. A reasonably satisfactory wage equation turned out to be of relatively simple structure; it contains only a two-period moving average of the change in the private consumption deflator (MAPCP) as a proxy for expected inflation, the rate of unemployment (UNR) and a dummy variable (DUMMY) for the second half of 1981 to the first half of 1983. Although the size of the estimated coefficient of the inflation variable should not be significantly different from unity on *a priori* grounds, it deviated considerably from unity in all of the tested specifications. Hence, the data appear to suggest a remarkable degree of money illusion in the Turkish economy. In order to derive a theoretically more plausible wage equation, i.e. a Phillips curve which is vertical in the long run, a unity coefficient was imposed on the price expectations variable. This led to the following wage equation (t-ratios are in brackets):

$$\begin{array}{llll} WR = 0.1898 & + 1.0000\ MAPCP & - 0.0236\ UNR & + 0.0560\ DUMMY \\ \quad (3.52) & \quad (\text{imposed}) & \quad (-4.10) & \quad (1.79) \end{array}$$

$$S.E.E. = 0.048 \qquad R^2 = 0.763$$

In order to derive the non-accelerating inflation rate of unemployment (NAIRU), a price equation has been estimated. The specification used is a cost mark-up price equation with an adaptive expectations mechanism. The most suitable model appeared to be the rate of change of the consumer price deflator (PCP) as a function of a three-period moving average of import price changes (MAPM), the rate of change of the unit labour cost (ULC), a proxy for demand pressure (PRESS) defined as the deviation of real GNP growth from a ten-period moving average and a dummy variable (DUMMY1) for the first half of 1975 to the first half of 1977. The sum of the coefficients of import prices and unit labour cost in the price equation were constrained to unity.

$$\begin{array}{lllll} PCP = 0.0444 & + 0.151\ MAPM & + 0.849\ ULC & - 1.2511\ PRESS & - 0.0773\ DUMMY1 \\ \quad (4.47) & \quad (1.97) & \quad (1.97) & \quad (-2.47) & \quad (-4.41) \end{array}$$

$$S.E.E. = 0.038 \qquad R^2 = 0.900$$

Long-run equilibrium of this simple wage-price block will be characterised by stable inflation, wage and productivity growth, and realised expectations. In the absence of equilibrium values for the determinants of the NAIRU, average growth rates for import prices, wages and unit labour cost have been used. Solving the wage-price block for the unemployment rate which is consistent with the above long-run wage-price equilibrium leads to an estimate of the so-defined NAIRU. On the basis of the equations presented here, the NAIRU for Turkey is about 8 per cent, i.e. it is about 4 percentage points below the measured actual unemployment rate (excluding seasonal unemployment in agriculture) in 1986.

NOTE

1. For the concept of hysteresis, see David Coe, (1985), *"Nominal Wages, the NAIRU and Wage Flexibility"*, OECD Economic Studies, No.5 Autumn.

Annex II

CONSTANT MARKET SHARE ANALYSIS OF EXPORT GROWTH

The constant market share analysis of export performance used in Part I of the Survey is a statistical technique aimed at the quantification of structural advantages or disadvantages inherent in the geographical or commodity composition (or both) of a country's exports. In order to identify structural influences on export performance, changes in a country's exports are split up into main components: the growth of its country/commodity- weighted export markets (i.e. the growth that it would have achieved if it had maintained its previous market shares in total exports demanded in its country/commodity markets in the period under review) and a residual export growth component (assumed to reflect changes in a country's competitiveness causing gains or losses in actual market shares relative to base period shares).

To single out the contributions of country and commodity distribution to export growth a "three-level" analysis was adopted which can be outlined using the following notation:

$X_{i.}$ = value of Turkey's exports of commodity i in period t – 1

$X^1_{i.}$ = value of Turkey's exports of commodity i in period t

$X_{.j}$ = value of Turkey's exports to country j in period t – 1

$X^1_{.j}$ = value of Turkey's exports to country j in period t

X_{ij} = value of Turkey's exports of commodity i to country j in period t – 1

g = percentage increase in total area exports from period t – 1 to period t

g_i = percentage increase in area exports of commodity i from period t – 1 to period t

g_{ij} = percentage increase in area exports of commodity i to country j from period t – 1 to period t

In the first step of the analysis, exports may be viewed as a single good destined for a single market. If Turkey maintained its share of this market, then exports would increase by $gX_{..}$ and the following identity holds:

(1) $$X^1_{..} - X_{..} = gX_{..} + (X^1_{..} - X_{..} - gX_{..})$$

Identity (1) divides the growth in Turkey's exports into a part ascribed to the increase in world exports and an unexplained residual, which indicates the competitiveness effect. Taking into account that exports are in fact quite a diverse set of commodities the application of identity (1) for commodity i leads to

(2) $$X^1_{i.} - X_{i.} = g_iX_{i.} + (X^1_{i.} - X_{i.} - g_iX_i)$$

and aggregated over all commodities i to

(3) $$X^1_{..} - X_{..} = \sum_i g_iX_i + \sum_i (X^1_{i.} - X_{i.} - g_iX_{i.})$$

$$= \underset{(a)}{(gX_{..})} + \sum_i \underset{(b)}{(g_i - g)X_{i.}} + \sum_i \underset{(c)}{(X^1_{i.} - X_{i.} - g_iX_{i.})}$$

Equation (3) represents a "two-level" analysis, in which the growth of Turkey's exports is broken into components:

a) The general rise in area exports;
b) The commodity composition of Turkey's exports in period t-1; and
c) A residual indicating the difference between Turkey's actual export increase and the hypothetical increase if Turkey had maintained its share of the exports of each commodity group.

Finally, exports are differentiated by destination as well as by commodity type. The identity analogous to (1) and (2) is

(4) $$X^1_{ij} - X_{ij} = g_{ij} + (X^1_{ij} - X_{ij} - g_{ij}X_{ij})$$

and aggregation over all i commodities and j countries yields

(5) $$X^1_{..} - X_{..} = \sum_i \sum_j g_{ij}X_{ij} + \sum_i \sum_j (X^1_{ij} - X_{ij} - g_{ij}X_{ij})$$

$$= \underset{(a)}{(gX_{..})} + \sum_{i} \underset{(b)}{(g_i - g)X_{i.}} + \sum_i \sum_j \underset{(c)}{(g_{ij} - g_i)X_{ij}}$$

$$+ \sum_i \sum_j \underset{(d)}{(X^1_{ij} - X_{ij} - g_{ij}X_{ij})}$$

Identity (5) represents a "three-level" disaggregation in which the increase in Turkey's exports is broken down into parts attributed to:

a) The general rise in world exports;
b) The commodity composition of Turkey's exports;
c) The country composition of Turkey's exports; and
d) A residual reflecting the difference between the actual export growth and the growth that would have occurred if Turkey had maintained its share of exports of each commodity to each country. If the residual is negative a failure to maintain market shares is indicated and vice versa.

Export performance analysis, as presented in the Survey, defines Turkey's export market growth as the sum of individual growth rates gij of 288 elementary markets (derived from the matrix of 18 commodity and 16 regional markets) weighted by their base-year shares of total Turkish exports. Unfortunately, available statistics do not allow a breakdown of volume country markets by commodity groups. The country/commodity market share analysis shown in the table and diagrams in the main body of the Survey therefore had to be based on exports in current dollar values. Thus, the results of the export performance analysis in value terms ought to be read with care since the estimated competitiveness terms are inevitably distorted by other factors. The figures should, therefore, be taken as a rough indication of the volume effects on Turkey's exports resulting from relative export price changes *vis-à-vis* its competitors.

Annex III

CALENDAR OF MAIN ECONOMIC EVENTS

1986

February

Income tax rebate rates are revised. Moreover, starting from January 1986, apart from wage- and salary-earners and pensioners who were the initial beneficiaries, farmers and the self-employed are also entitled to tax rebates. For tax-payers assessed on a lump-sum basis, the rebate will be payable every two months; in the case of annual tax declarations, refunds will be made at the end of the year. New rates are:

Monthly expenditures	Rebate rates (per cent)
Up to TL 60 000:	
first TL 30 000	20
above	15
Up to TL 100 000:	
first TL 60 000	17.5
above	10
Up to TL 360 000:	
first TL 100 000	14.5
above	5
Up to TL 720 000:	
first TL 360 000	20
above	15
Up to TL 1 200 000:	
first TL 720 000	17.5
above	10
Over TL 1 200 000:	
first TL 1 200 000	14
above	5

March

Commercial banks' interest rates on deposits are lowered from 45 to 44 per cent for 3-month time deposits, and from 50 to 48 per cent for 6-month deposits.

The reserve ratio for commercial banks is reduced from 18 to 15 per cent, effective from 1st March 1986, instead of September 1986 as initially announced.

Commercial banks are directed to set the buying and selling rates for foreign exchange within a band of 1 per cent below and above the rates announced by the Central Bank.

The ratio of commercial banks' foreign currency holdings that must be transferred to the Central Bank is reduced from 20 to 15 per cent, as is the reserve ratio on foreign currency deposits.

On 14th March, the Turkish lira is devalued by 5 per cent against the US dollar.

April

The tax rebate on cotton yarn exports is abolished.

Withholding tax on interest earned from government bonds and from foreign currency deposits – introduced in December 1985 – is reduced from 5 per cent to zero, and from 1 per cent to zero, respectively.

The Central Bank introduces a system for inter-bank lending. Short-term inter-bank loans can normally be made for periods of one to two weeks, exceptionally 21 days. Each participating bank determines its operations limit and deposits a collateral equal to 130 per cent of the limit with the Central Bank. Overnight transactions are to be introduced at a later stage.

The banking and insurance tax rate on inter-bank transactions is reduced from 3 to 1 per cent.

Interest rates for deposits with commercial banks are changed:

	Annual rates (per cent)	
	Old	New
Sight deposits	5	11.6
Time deposits:		
One month	35	35
Three months	44	42
Six months	48	45
One year	55	52

After 1st August 1986, the rate for sight deposits will equal two-thirds of the going one-month rate.

The surcharge on exports of cereals is abolished.

May

The 1986 Import Regime is further liberalised. The number of items subject to licence is reduced from 245 to 100.

Exemptions granted to public sector entities (e.g. municipalities and SEEs) in respect of customs duties, some other taxes, and fees on imports are abolished.

With an amendment in the Tobacco Law, the tobacco monopoly is lifted. Cigarettes can now be manufactured by local or foreign private firms, but prices will be set by the Monopoly Administration. Importation of tobacco, subject to a surcharge, is also liberalised.

June

A 5 per cent charge on the cif value of imports from EEC countries is abolished.

July

Commercial banks' interest rates on deposits are lowered from 35 to 30 per cent for 1-month deposits and from 42 to 40 per cent for 3-month deposits.

Support prices for raisins are increased by 46.6 per cent and for figs by 41.7 per cent.

Import guarantee deposit rates – which had been reduced at the beginning of the year – are increased from 3 to 9 per cent and from 1 to 7 per cent, to be effective from 1st July 1986.

August

A "Tobacco Production Board" is set up to regulate cultivation areas and types of tobacco grown. Private firms may operate tobacco factories in partnership with the Monopoly Administration.

October

The surcharge of $1/kg. on cotton exports is abolished. Premiums of TL 100/kg. and TL 170/kg. will be paid to exporters for Aegean and Cukurova cotton respectively.

The surcharge of $5/ton on tobacco exports is abolished.

The 10 per cent surcharge for the Resource Utilisation Support Fund on export credits is abolished.

The regulation restricting trade with countries under a state trading regime to Turkish companies whose exports have exceeded $50 million during the preceding year is abolished.

Surcharges are increased on imports of specific luxury goods.

The 1987 official support price for tobacco is increased by 55 per cent.

Prices of monopoly products are increased by 15 to 60 per cent.

Rules governing the establishment of non-bank foreign exchange agencies are published. The minimum capital requirement is TL 1 billion, of which at least half must be paid up. Agencies must have at least ten branches. Buying and selling rates may be set at 1 per cent above the Central Bank rates and a commission may be charged.

The Central Bank decreases rediscount rate on short-term credits from 52 to 48 per cent.

Commercial banks' minimum interest rates on deposits are lowered from 30 to 29 per cent on one-month deposits, from 40 to 36 per cent on three-month deposits, and from 52 to 48 per cent on one-year deposits.

November

Joint-stock companies which have not declared losses in the last three years are permitted to issue bonds above current ceilings subject to agreement by the Capital Market Board. Commercial paper with one year maturity may not exceed one-half of the bond-issue ceiling. The total amount of security issues – bonds, commercial paper or promissory notes – cannot exceed the ceiling allowed for bonds.

A series of policy measures is introduced in November and December aimed at restricting growth of domestic demand and promoting exports:

- The Government is authorised to raise VAT to 15 per cent; as a first step the current rate is increased to 12 per cent, to be effective from 1st December 1986; the zero rate for basic foodstuffs is maintained, and a rate of 1 per cent is introduced for some agricultural goods;
- The Central Bank rediscount facility for short-term export credits is made operative; credits to firms whose exports in the last three years were not less than $5 million will be eligible for rediscount at the Central Bank at a rate of 38 per cent up to four months' maturity, within an overall limit of 25 per cent of the fob value of committed exports;

December

- Export tax rebates are also reintroduced. Rates vary from 2 per cent (for fruit and vegetables) to 8 per cent (manufactured goods). An additional rebate is granted for exports exceeding specific limits: premiums of 2 per cent for exports between $2-10 million, 4 per cent for exports between $10-30 million, and 6 per cent for exports above $30 million;
- The surcharge earmarked for the Price Stability and Support Fund and levied on the cif value of imports is increased from 2 to 4 per cent. The Fund's scope for supporting exports is enlarged;
- Customs duties on 163 items are lowered by 50 to 100 per cent; moreover, the items are included in the "import list subject to surcharge"; import surcharges on several goods are increased;
- The motor-vehicle purchase tax is increased by 100 per cent, and motor-vehicle tax by 50 per cent.
- The income tax law is amended; ceilings for taxation on a lump-sum basis are raised 100 per cent.

Rules announced in November governing private bond issues are amended. Joint-stock companies with a minimum capital of TL 2 billion become eligible for issuing commercial paper up to 12 months' maturity. The total value of commercial paper issued may not exceed the ceiling allowed for bond issues. The Capital Market Board decides whether a bank guarantee will be required.

The Import Regime is further liberalised. The number of items on the list "subject to import permission" is reduced from 245 to 111. Guarantee deposit rates are fixed uniformly at 7 per cent.

Interest rates for one-month deposits are lowered from 29 to 28 per cent and for one-year deposits from 48 to 45 per cent.

The 1987 Budget is approved by Parliament. Total appropriatons are foreseen to rise by 35 per cent to TL 109 trillion.

1987

January

A decree regulating the operation of chartered accountants is published. Auditor firms must be in the form of a joint-stock company, with a capital of at least TL 100 million, and will have to obtain a licence from the Undersecretariat of the Treasury and Foreign Trade. Banks must be be audited by these officially approved auditors.

The interest rate for credits eligible for support by the Foreign Credit Exchange Rate Differential Fund is reduced from 35 to 32 per cent.

February

The advance support price for wheat is increased by TL 4/kg. to TL 92/kg.

The Central Bank directs commercial banks to reduce interest rates on one-year deposits from 45 to 43 per cent.

The Central Bank law is amended. The Bank is authorised to engage in open market operations. The securities acceptable for these operations are: Treasury bonds, registered bonds and commercial paper issued by joint-stock companies, certificates of deposit issued by banks, revenue-sharing certificates, and other bonds issued by government agencies.

Private companies are permitted to operate electrical power plants in conformity with the Government's energy programme.

Central government administrations are ordered to cut 1987 Budget appropriations by 8 per cent, with the exception of personnel expenditures.

March

An "Agricultural Reform Fund" is established. The Fund shall extend credits to farmers for the purchase of equipment or inputs up to five years. Housing credits to farmers who are resettled in new regions will be of 20 years' maturity. The Fund will obtain its resources from Budget transfers and the proceeds from the sale or leasing of Treasury land.

Subject to government authorisation, creditor banks are permitted to swap bad loans against equity in companies in financial difficulties and take over control of their boards. These transactions are exempt from stamp duty and banking and insurance tax; interest earnings converted into capital are exempt from corporation income tax. But banks' shareholdings exceeding 15 per cent of equity must be relinquished up to the year 1999. The law also provides for a graduated reduction on standard corporation tax (46 per cent) if ownership in joint-stock companies is more widely dispersed. The tax rate will be as low as 30 per cent, if 80 per cent of equity is held by at least 200 persons, each owning less than 1 per cent of the shares.

The same law authorises the State Investment Bank to operate as an export-import financing bank. The Bank will insure and guarantee imports and exports of goods and services, including overseas contracting, and Turkish investments abroad.

April

The Wage Negotiations Co-ordination Board, which was formed in 1982 to set guidelines for collective bargaining agreements, is abolished.

Extra-budgetary funds set up under special laws in order to speed up implementation of certain public sector programmes are made subject to parliamentary supervision. At the time of budget discussions in Parliament, the Funds' proposed budget and final accounts of the preceding year will be discussed and approved by a special committee.

May

Turkish contractors successful in international bidding for public sector projects financed by foreign credits are eligible for tax rebate of 2 per cent of the foreign exchange cost of the contract value.

Surcharges and customs duty on imports of selected investment goods are lowered.

By decree, new incentives are provided for farmers:
- The Agricultural Bank and the Agricultural Credit Co-operatives are authorised to extend operational credits (up to TL 600 000 and without a mortgage guarantee) at an interest rate of 22 per cent. The cost of the interest differential compared to market interest rate will be borne by the Treasury;
- Dairy farmers are granted an incentive premium of TL 35 per litre of milk sold. The cost of subsidy will be met from the Support and Price Stability Fund;
- 20 per cent of the cost of the insecticide used in farming will be refunded from the Support and Price Stability Fund;
- The subsidy on animal feed is increased from 20 to 25 per cent.

STATISTICAL ANNEX

Table A. **National product**

TL billion

	Current prices									
	1977	1978	1979	1980	1981	1982	1983	1984	1985	1986[1]
Agriculture, forestry, fishing	219.8	301.3	465.8	925.0	1 325.6	1 678.9	2 118.0	3 397.1	4 790.3	6 484.8
Industry	158.0	273.4	479.9	1 024.2	1 572.3	2 191.5	3 096.4	5 116.1	8 060.5	11 365.1
Construction	42.1	64.0	103.9	213.0	285.4	357.0	447.6	697.4	951.2	1 410.5
Wholesale and retail trade	107.0	165.9	301.8	650.8	1 011.5	1 370.1	1 906.6	3 139.9	4 397.0	6 027.2
Transports and communications	72.2	110.1	199.6	421.1	623.6	841.9	1 136.3	1 785.4	2 711.2	3 644.5
Financial institutions	20.2	25.9	36.4	71.9	130.0	157.0	203.3	466.6	739.8	1 027.1
Ownership of dwellings	34.1	53.7	86.0	191.9	262.5	351.1	450.2	725.6	1 055.6	1 509.0
Private professions and services	41.2	62.6	106.8	222.4	332.0	446.2	598.0	570.6	1 379.6	1 906.5
Government, health, education	101.5	133.1	235.2	377.7	481.1	686.6	860.9	1 056.4	1 441.0	2 073.3
Gross domestic product at factor costs	796.1	1 190.1	2 015.3	4 098.0	6 024.0	8 080.8	10 871.6	16 949.1	25 526.1	35 448.1
Net income from abroad	9.9	15.9	43.6	107.2	140.0	114.6	20.1	162.8	237.6	21.8
Indirect taxes minus subsidies	66.8	84.7	140.6	230.0	389.6	539.6	714.4	863.0	2 025.7	3 720.6
Gross national product at market prices	872.8	1 290.7	2 199.5	4 435.2	6 553.6	8 735.0	11 551.9	17 974.8	27 789.4	39 190.5
	1968 prices									
	1977	1978	1979	1980	1981	1982	1983	1984	1985	1986[1]
Agriculture, forestry, fishing	42.2	43.3	44.5	45.3	45.3	48.2	48.1	49.8	51.0	55.0
Industry	43.1	46.0	43.4	40.8	43.9	46.0	49.7	54.7	58.1	63.4
Construction	11.8	12.3	12.8	12.9	12.9	13.0	13.1	13.3	13.7	14.9
Wholesale and retail trade	26.4	27.4	26.8	26.2	28.1	29.4	31.4	33.9	35.5	38.7
Transports and communications	19.0	19.5	18.6	18.5	18.7	19.1	19.7	21.2	22.2	23.2
Financial institutions	4.6	4.8	4.9	5.0	5.1	5.2	5.2	5.5	5.6	5.9
Ownership of dwellings	8.8	9.2	9.5	9.9	10.2	10.5	10.8	11.1	11.3	11.7
Private professions and services	9.4	9.5	9.4	9.3	9.8	10.2	10.6	11.2	11.8	12.8
Government, health, education	17.5	18.6	19.4	20.5	21.4	22.5	23.5	24.1	24.9	25.8
Gross domestic product at factor costs	182.7	190.6	189.5	188.5	195.3	204.2	212.1	224.9	234.3	251.3
Net income from abroad	1.8	1.9	2.9	2.2	1.8	1.0	0.1	0.6	0.6	0.1
Indirect taxes minus subsidies	18.9	16.7	16.0	15.4	17.5	19.3	19.7	20.2	23.3	27.5
Gross national product at market prices	203.4	209.2	208.3	206.1	214.7	224.4	231.9	245.6	258.2	278.9

1. Provisional.
Source: State Planning Organisation, *Main Economic Indicators.*

Table B. **Supply and use of resources**

Percentage volume change over previous year

	1977	1978	1979	1980	1981	1982	1983	1984	1985	1986[2]
Gross value added:										
Agriculture, forestry and fishing	–1.3	2.7	2.8	1.7	0.1	6.4	–0.1	3.5	2.4	7.7
Industry	10.2	6.6	–5.6	–6.0	7.4	4.9	8.0	10.1	6.3	9.0
Mining	39.2	26.7	–16.3	–4.1	–7.3	–5.5	7.5	7.9	11.9	–4.6
Manufacturing	7.3	3.6	–5.3	–6.4	9.5	5.4	8.7	10.2	5.5	9.8
Energy	10.6	12.4	8.0	–4.5	7.0	11.6	2.2	11.1	7.8	15.5
Construction	5.5	4.2	4.2	0.8	0.4	0.5	0.6	1.9	2.9	8.3
Wholesale and retail trade	4.9	4.0	–2.3	–2.4	7.4	4.6	6.9	8.0	4.6	9.1
Transports and communications	6.6	2.5	–4.4	–0.6	0.9	2.2	3.2	7.7	4.8	4.2
Financial institutions	9.7	5.0	3.0	1.8	1.9	1.6	0.5	4.5	3.5	3.7
Ownership of dwellings	3.8	4.0	3.9	4.1	2.7	2.7	2.8	2.8	2.6	3.8
Private professions and services	6.4	1.2	–0.9	–1.0	4.4	4.8	3.5	6.1	4.9	8.8
Government, health, education	6.0	6.2	4.2	5.8	4.0	5.4	4.2	2.6	3.3	3.7
Gross domestic product at factor cost	4.9	4.3	–0.6	–0.5	3.6	4.5	3.9	6.0	4.2	7.3
Gross national product at market prices	3.9	2.9	–0.4	–1.1	4.1	4.5	3.3	5.9	5.1	8.0
Foreign balance[1]	(–1.4)	(9.2)	(2.0)	(0.2)	(2.5)	(1.7)	(–1.3)	(0.3)	(0.6)	(–2.9)
Total domestic demand	4.5	–5.4	–2.2	–1.2	1.6	2.8	4.7	5.4	4.4	10.9
Fixed capital investment	3.9	–10.0	–3.6	–10.0	1.7	3.5	3.0	5.5	12.5	13.8
Public	11.0	–13.7	4.6	–3.7	9.4	2.2	1.9	3.3	16.0	13.7
Private	–2.7	–6.0	–11.6	–17.3	–8.7	5.5	4.7	8.7	7.8	13.8
Stock changes[1]	(–0.1)	(–1.7)	(0.6)	(3.9)	(0.8)	(–1.0)	(0.2)	(0.4)	(–0.5)	(0.4)
Consumption	5.0	–2.4	–2.5	–3.4	0.6	3.9	4.7	4.9	3.0	9.6
Public	3.2	9.9	1.7	8.8	0.9	2.0	1.7	3.0	3.2	8.8
Private	5.2	–3.9	–3.1	–5.2	0.6	4.2	5.0	5.1	3.0	9.7

1. Contribution to GNP growth.
2. Provisional.

Source: State Planning Organisation, *Main Economic Indicators.*

Table C. **Agricultural production**

	Units	1977	1978	1979	1980	1981	1982	1983	1984	1985	1986
Cereals:	1 000 tons										
Wheat		16 650	16 700	17 500	16 500	17 000	17 500	16 400	17 200	17 000	19 000
Barley		4 750	4 750	5 240	5 300	5 900	6 400	5 425	6 500	6 500	7 000
Maize		1 265	1 300	1 350	1 240	1 200	1 360	1 480	1 500	1 900	2 300
Rye		690	620	620	525	530	430	380	360	360	350
Other		857	867	817	849	780	841	807	719	625	708
Pulses		813	729	762	810	873	1 230	1 370	1 312	1 467	1 925
Industrial crops:											
Sugar beet		8 995	8 837	8 760	6 766	11 165	12 732	12 770	11 108	9 830	10 662
Tobacco		248	297	217	234	168	210	186	178	170	170
Cotton		575	475	476	500	488	488	520	602	577	531
Oilseeds		1 517	1 374	1 511	1 653	1 356	1 507	1 690	1 843	1 961	2 095
Wool		55	57	59	62	64	62	..	..	..	..
Fruits and nuts:											
Grapes		3 180	3 496	3 500	3 600	3 700	3 650	3 400	3 300	3 300	3 000
Figs		175	185	200	205	250	280	330	330	340	370
Hazelnuts		290	310	300	250	350	220	392	300	180	300
Citrus fruit		1 147	1 081	1 147	1 182	1 225	1 235	1 299	1 334	983	1 133
Livestock:	Thousands										
Cattle (inc. buffalo)		15 552	15 964	16 580	17 017	16 983	15 295	14 857	12 954	..	..
Sheep and goats		60 984	62 389	64 801	64 222	68 524	67 849	65 439	54 031	..	..
Poultry		50 964	54 711	58 941	60 240	58 834	60 945	63 597	63 760	..	..

Source: State Planning Organisation, ***Main Economic Indicators.***

Table D. **Industrial production**

	Units	1978	1979	1980	1981	1982	1983	1984	1985	1986[1]
Mining, fuel, energy: selected products	1 000 tons									
Coals		7 741	7 200	6 598	7 285	7 223	6 725	7 103	7 260	7 008
Lignite (ungrated)		18 030	15 603	16 998	18 951	20 542	23 847	27 199	39 437	45 321
Chrome ore		670	586	551	574	618	515	688	877	. .
Iron ore		4 198	1 955	2 579	2 876	3 072	3 723	4 049	3 420	. .
Copper		13	22	16	27	26	19	32	34	36
Crude petroleum		2 736	2 845	2 330	2 364	2 333	2 203	2 087	2 110	2 346
Petroleum products		11 237	10 182	11 732	12 388	15 267	14 764	16 460	16 456	. .
Electricity	Billion kWh	22	23	23	25	26	27	30	34	40
Manufacturing: selected products:	1 000 t									
Crude iron		1 569	1 901	1 810	1 727	2 102	2 645	2 792	3 094	3 578
Steel ingots		1 628	1 789	1 700	1 744	1 998	2 479	2 753	3 080	3 596
Sheets and pipes		399	402	419	433	526	676	928	920	1 019
Cement		15 344	13 784	12 875	15 043	15 778	13 595	15 738	17 581	20 004
Coke		1 865	2 096	1 928	1 875	2 102	2 501	2 501	2 604	. .
Superphosphate		820	952	1 723	2 485	1 893	2 446	2 881	2 348	. .
Glass		178	169	108	243	303	293	378	351	. .
Paper and cardboard		304	301	301	365	398	393	488	470	. .
Sugar		1 009	972	1 049	1 117	1 723	1 714	2 554	2 859	. .
Woollen and cotton yarns	Million meters	188	232	197	264	282	299	333	. .	. .
Woollen and cotton fabrics		488	480	425	503	523	575	597	. .	. .

1. Provisional.
Source: State Planning Organisation, *Main Economic Indicators.*

Table E. **Prices**

Annual percentage change

	1976	1977	1978	1979	1980	1981	1982	1983	1984	1985	1986
Wholesale prices (1963 = 100)[1]											
General index	15.7	23.9	52.6	63.9	107.2	36.8	25.2	30.6	52.0	40.0	26.7
Food and feeding stuff	15.0	22.8	45.0	48.9	100.3	41.6	21.2	26.4	61.3	36.7	23.4
Raw materials and semi-finished goods	16.6	26.3	65.7	87.5	115.7	31.1	30.2	35.4	41.9	44.2	30.2
Consumer price index (1963 = 100)[1]											
Ankara	16.6	22.5	53.2	61.8	101.4	33.9	28.3	30.8	47.3	44.9	35.2
Istanbul	17.4	25.8	61.9	63.5	94.2	37.6	32.7	28.8	45.6	45.0	34.8
GNP deflator	16.7	24.5	43.7	71.1	105.7	41.9	27.2	28.0	49.9	43.6	30.6
Foreign trade prices (TL)											
Export prices	13.8	25.2	43.1	59.6	172.8	38.9	43.8	21.8	64.8	44.3	20.8
Import prices	12.4	23.4	54.9	67.7	231.0	46.7	44.6	31.0	63.9	44.1	10.5

1. Old series; new price indices have recently been published, see Table 4.
Source: State Institute of Statistics, *Price Indices Monthly Bulletin.*

Table F. **Imports by commodities**[1]

$ million

	1977	1978	1979	1980	1981	1982	1983	1984	1985	1986
I. *Agriculture and livestock*	112	50	36	50	125	176	138	417	375	457
II. *Mining and quarrying*	1 546	1 486	1 818	4 006	4 098	3 961	3 864	3 908	4 186	2 440
Oil	1 436	1 396	1 712	3 862	3 878	3 749	3 665	3 637	3 612	2 008
Crude oil	1 152	1 044	962	2 952	3 258	3 528	3 242	3 373	3 321	1 808
Oil products	284	352	750	910	620	221	423	264	291	200
Other	110	90	106	144	220	212	199	271	574	432
III. *Industrial products*	4 037	2 943	3 092	3 759	4 641	4 657	5 177	6 432	7 052	8 302
Agriculture-based processed products	58	50	115	301	228	176	203	434	481	480
Industrial products	3 978	2 893	2 977	3 458	4 412	4 482	4 974	5 998	6 565	7 822
Chemicals	555	476	524	727	919	839	1 032	1 212	1 294	1 301
Fertilizer	214	283	356	395	280	51	119	128	..	121
Rubber and plastics	266	154	145	181	240	237	251	359	343	372
Textiles	51	50	46	79	78	103	98	117	146	161
Glass and ceramics	25	18	28	35	40	34	57	63	63	96
Iron and steel	690	408	345	462	605	591	675	862	1 060	1 028
Non-ferrous metals	97	42	55	87	141	122	195	220	224	230
Metal products	15	20	14	23	23	37	30	34	38	51
Machinery	1 060	761	903	843	1 223	1 309	1 432	1 618	1 551	2 304
Electrical appliances	291	218	251	270	336	374	398	573	664	892
Motor vehicles	572	378	221	223	356	594	478	517	812	768
Other industrial products	141	83	88	133	171	191	209	295	370	498
IV. *Imports with waiver*	102	120	123	94	69	49	56	..	..	..
Total	5 797	4 599	5 069	7 909	8 933	8 843	9 235	10 757	11 613	11 199

1. Excluding transit trade.
Source: State Institute of Statistics. *Monthly Indicators.*

Table G. **Exports by commodities**[1]

$ million

	1977	1978	1979	1980	1981	1982	1983	1984	1985	1986
I. *Agricultural products*	1 041	1 542	1 344	1 672	2 219	2 141	1 881	1 749	1 719	1 886
Cereals	120	262	167	181	326	337	376	267	234	246
Fruits and vegetables	440	561	647	754	795	649	591	646	561	820
Hazelnuts	251	331	353	395	302	241	246	305	255	378
Dried fruit	100	145	166	187	208	168	120	119	73	177
Citrus fruit	77	44	53	86	125	77	72	62	58	74
Other	12	41	75	86	160	163	153	160	175	191
Industrial crops and forestry products	432	617	446	606	813	741	531	492	659	495
Cotton	210	348	227	323	348	297	197	168	170	139
Tobacco	176	225	176	234	395	348	238	216	330	270
Other	46	44	43	49	70	96	96	108	159	86
Live animals and sea products	49	102	84	131	285	414	382	343	265	325
II. *Mining and quarrying products*	126	124	132	191	194	175	189	240	244	247
III. *Processed and manufactured products*	586	622	785	1 047	2 290	3 430	3 658	5 144	5 995	5 324
Processed agricultural products	137	110	151	209	412	569	670	808	647	667
Manufactured products	449	512	634	838	1 878	2 861	2 988	4 336	5 348	4 657
Textiles and clothing	260	309	378	424	803	1 056	1 299	1 875	1 790	1 851
Hides and leather	52	40	44	50	82	111	192	401	484	345
Forestry	1	1	2	4	20	33	15	24	106	52
Chemicals	34	24	23	76	94	148	120	173	266	350
Rubber and plastics	3	2	3	16	72	60	77	97	108	141
Petroleum products	–	–	–	39	107	343	232	409	372	178
Glass and ceramics	27	30	37	36	102	104	108	146	190	158
Cement	9	41	45	40	198	207	81	56	44	27
Iron and steel	14	21	31	34	100	362	407	576	969	804
Non-ferrous metals	20	12	15	18	30	45	79	86	116	111
Metal products and machinery	14	18	18	30	85	143	122	134	450	263
Electrical equipment and products	3	4	4	11	26	75	69	100	119	130
Other	12	10	34	60	159	174	187	259	334	247
Total	1 753	2 288	2 261	2 910	4 703	5 746	5 728	7 133	7 958	7 457

1. Excluding transit trade.

Source: State Institute of Statistics, *Monthly Indicators*.

Table H(*a*). **Balance of payments**[1]

$ million

	1974	1975	1976	1977	1978	1979	1980	1981	1982	1983
Current account										
Trade balance	–2 245	–3 337	–3 169	–4 044	–2 311	–2 808	–4 999	–4 230	–3 097	–3 507
Exports fob	1 532	1 401	1 960	1 753	2 288	2 261	2 910	4 703	5 746	5 727
Imports cif	3 777	4 738	5 129	5 797	4 599	5 069	7 909	8 933	8 843	9 235
Invisibles, net	1 526	1 458	867	657	792	1 105	1 319	1 888	1 830	1 314
Workers' remittances	1 426	1 312	982	982	983	1 694	2 071	2 490	2 187	1 554
Interest payments[2]	–103	–124	–217	–320	–489	–1 010	–1 138	–1 443	–1 566	–1 512
Profit transfers	–71	–36	–83	–116	–47	–42	–51	–56	–43	–57
Tourism, net	42	46	–27	–65	145	179	212	277	262	284
Other, net	232	260	212	176	200	284	225	620	990	1 045
Current balance	–719	–1 879	–2 302	–3 387	–1 519	– 1 703	–3 680	–2 342	–1 267	–2 193
Capital account										
Private capital	146	251	360	1 243	728	–160	313	–18	119	493
Imports with waiver	58	99	136	102	120	124	95	69	49	56
Direct investment	33	55	27	67	47	86	53	60	55	72
Commercial credits[3]	55	97	197	1 074	561	–370	165	–147	15	365
Official capital	300	417	576	503	855	1 845	3 585	2 332	2 590	2 117
Project credits	268	382	570	499	450	421	547	642	754	508
Programme credits	2	6	6	4	110	500	1 588	840	1 086	609
Debt relief	30	29	–	–	295	924	1 450	850	750	1 000
Principal	30	29	–	–	195	460	980	600	650	930
Interest	–	–	–	–	100	464	470	250	100	70
Debt repayments[2]	–156	–147	–119	–214	–451	–945	–1 556	–1 185	–1 502	–2 023
Capital balance	290	521	817	1 532	1 132	740	2 342	1 129	1 207	587
Basic balance	–429	–1 358	–1 485	–1 855	–387	–963	–1 338	–1 213	–60	–1 606
SDR allocations	–	27	18	–	–	27	27	24	–	–
Short-term credits	–63	939	1 895	1 762	421	194	216	–212	74	755
Errors and omissions	138	–311	–446	–473	–47	818	941	1 124	206	613
Overall balance	–354	–703	18	–566	–13	76	–154	–277	220	238
Financing:										
Net use of IMF resources	–	216	130	–	170	8	461	335	205	193
Net change in reserves (increase –)	354	487	–148	566	–157	–84	–307	–58	–425	–53

1. In 1984, the Central Bank of Turkey changed the presentation of the balance of payments. The new series are given in Table H(*b*).
2. Before debt relief.
3. Inclusive of acceptance credits.

Source: Central Bank of Turkey, *Monthly Statistics*.

Table H(b). **Balance of payments**

$ million

	1981	1982	1983	1984	1985	1986*
Trade balance[1]	–3 864	–2 628	–2 990	–2 942	–2 975	–3 081
Exports (fob)	4 703	5 890	5 905	7 389	8 255	7 583
Imports (fob)	8 567	8 518	8 895	10 331	11 230	10 664
Invisibles, net	1 945	1 692	1 092	1 535	1 962	1 553
Services	–630	–602	–693	–579	–36	–396
Tourism	277	224	292	271	770	637
Investment income	–1 434	–1 473	–1 449	–1 387	–1 321	–1 664
Interest payments[2]	–1 442	–1 565	–1 511	–1 586	–1 753	–2 134
Other	8	92	62	199	432	470
Other services	527	647	464	537	515	631
Transfers	2 575	2 294	1 785	2 114	1 998	1 949
Official[3]	16	105	236	229	236	246
Private	2 559	2 189	1 549	1 885	1 762	1 703
Workers' remittances	2 490	2 140	1 513	1 807	1 714	1 634
Other[4]	69	49	36	78	48	69
Current balance	–1 919	–936	–1 898	–1 407	–1 013	–1 528
Long-term capital, net	1 263	1 085	349	1 159	75	650
Direct investment	95	55	46	113	98	125
Credits received	1 538	1 882	1 299	2 150	1 835	2 670
Project credits	642	754	508	733	926	1 296
Other official credits[5]	840	982	535	873	280	723
Private credits	56	146	256	544	629	651
Debt relief	850	750	1 000	580	–	–
Principal	600	650	930	580	–	–
Interest	250	100	70	–	–	–
Debt repayments[2]	–1 220	–1 602	–1 996	–1 684	–1 858	–2 145
Official	..	..	..	..	–1 711	–1 735
Private	..	..	..	..	–147	–410
Basic balance	–656	149	–1 549	–248	–938	–878
Short-term capital	–307	–83	1 033	36	1 656	1 478
Errors and omissions	478	–75	507	317	–818	–65
Counterpart items	68	13	161	–171	223	251
Overall balance	–417	168	152	–66	123	786
Change in official reserves	417	–168	–152	66	–123	–786
Net use of IMF	268	133	112	–141	–103	–241
Other	149	–301	–264	207	–20	–545

* Provisional.
1. Including transit trade.
2. Before debt relief.
3. Including grants.
4. Including workers' imports.
5. Including European Resettlement Fund loans, World Bank Structural Adjustment loans and bilateral programme loans.

Source: Central Bank of Turkey, *Monthly Statistics.*

Table I. **Money and banking**

End of period
TL million

	1977	1978	1979	1980	1981	1982	1983	1984	1985	1986
Money supply:										
M1	209.1	283.6	444.5	704.0	972.0	1 341.9	1 941.0	2 252.7	3 208.7	4 361.7
Notes and coins	63.0	93.8	143.7	217.5	280.6	411.9	547.5	735.5	1 011.4	1 585.8
Sight deposits	145.3	189.3	298.2	483.5	686.9	926.7	1 374.0	1 485.4	2 177.4	2 763.1
Deposits with Central Bank	0.8	0.5	2.6	3.1	4.5	3.3	19.5	31.8	19.9	12.8
M2	243.5	328.0	527.8	881.9	1 637.2	2 554.1	3 288.4	5 179.0	8 145.5	10 252.1
Time deposits	34.4	44.4	83.3	155.7	514.6	954.6	1 232.6	2 652.5	4 263.5	5 122.8
Certificates of deposits	–	–	–	22.2	150.5	257.6	113.8	273.8	673.3	767.6
M3	275.4	383.4	609.4	1 071.9	2 140.2	3 174.1	3 978.7	5 933.7	9 185.1	. .
Other quasi money	31.9	55.4	81.6	190.0	503.0	620.0	690.3	754.7	1 039.6	. .
Central Bank										
Deposits, total	62.9	99.5	144.1	266.9	673.0	866.4	993.0	1 278.8	1 630.4	1 749.1
Public sector	3.3	2.7	7.6	51.7	272.5	303.7	209.6	68.9	139.1	123.0
Banks	56.4	79.7	110.9	158.1	323.7	462.2	645.5	1 061.9	1 455.6	1 561.6
IMF and counterpart of aid	2.4	13.1	13.6	40.1	74.3	97.3	134.5	113.6	0.9	1.3
Other	0.8	4.0	12.0	17.0	2.5	2.7	3.4	34.4	34.6	63.2
Credits, total	189.7	241.9	382.1	655.2	925.5	910.5	1 234.1	879.9	1 299.6	1 610.6
Treasury	45.2	56.6	91.7	188.7	261.9	266.2	338.6	528.4	794.5	967.5
State Economic Enterprises	46.5	67.6	122.7	178.2	233.3	256.4	250.5	36.9	122.4	162.6
State Investment Bank	35.0	39.3	45.2	45.7	45.6	44.0	41.8	0	49.7	77.4
Deposit money banks	38.3	55.0	75.8	149.8	264.7	301.3	541.5	278.9	290.8	368.1
Agricultural co-operatives	24.7	23.4	46.7	92.8	120.0	42.6	61.7	35.7	42.1	35.0
Deposit money banks										
Deposits, total	205.8	269.1	432.4	745.5	1 509.5	2 357.4	3 083.2	4 980.8	7 998.9	10 390.3
Public	26.0	35.3	50.9	84.1	157.4	218.5	361.7	516.1	884.7	. .
Private	179.8	233.8	381.5	661.4	1 352.1	2 138.9	2 721.5	4 464.7	7 114.2	. .
Lending, total	238.3	296.3	446.2	789.5	1 318.7	1 800.5	2 417.5	3 149.3	5 567.9	7 683.2
Public	37.6	43.4	76.1	148.7	160.2	167.1	216.3	220.8	707.3	. .
Private	200.7	252.9	370.1	640.8	1 158.5	1 633.4	2 201.2	2 928.5	4 860.6	. .
Investment and development banks										
Lending, total	84.3	105.4	135.4	169.8	245.2	345.4	428.2	535.0	646.0	1 008.1
Public	75.2	90.8	109.3	121.4	172.5	239.5	281.9	299.3	330.7	. .
Private	9.1	14.6	26.1	48.4	72.7	105.9	146.3	235.7	315.3	. .
Total bank lending (net of Central Bank advances to the banks)	414.2	526.0	796.1	1 326.3	2 059.1	2 668.6	3 426.4	4 231.8	7 114.8	9 821.5
Public	204.4	258.5	399.9	637.1	827.9	929.3	1 087.3	1 067.7	1 938.8	. .
Private	209.8	267.6	396.2	689.2	1 231.2	1 739.3	2 339.1	3 164.1	5176.0	. .

Source: Central Bank of Turkey, *Monthly Statistics.*

Table J. **Workers' remittances by month**

$ million

	1977	1978	1979	1980	1981	1982	1983	1984	1985	1986
January	75.4	42.4	83.1	83.3	134.9	149.2	121.2	83.4	151.9	97.6
February	69.4	43.4	75.4	173.3	143.5	130.8	105.7	98.5	134.1	100.3
March	70.6	73.5	55.7	111.7	139.7	147.3	129.3	98.7	122.8	91.1
April	67.7	55.5	128.6	114.8	159.1	152.4	117.1	81.7	123.1	118.7
May	76.7	61.6	639.3	103.2	162.1	160.1	107.7	119.2	128.5	106.1
June	94.3	66.0	106.2	155.0	212.4	165.6	109.9	139.8	98.3	121.4
July	106.2	87.2	100.9	279.4	313.2	246.4	164.0	233.8	216.0	216.6
August	109.1	109.3	111.4	279.5	377.7	300.9	191.6	242.3	182.8	192.4
September	92.1	119.2	110.7	207.3	266.4	196.5	139.7	172.9	183.5	183.7
October	81.3	130.0	90.5	205.1	211.8	203.6	140.3	160.2	162.3	166.3
November	63.7	95.8	99.5	172.6	183.2	143.0	103.4	267.4	136.6	137.6
December	75.4	99.2	93.2	185.9	185.7	190.7	123.8	183.3	134.4	164.2
Total	981.9	983.1	1 694.5	2 071.1	2 489.7	2 186.5	1 553.7	1 881.2	1 774.3	1 696.0

Source: Central Bank of Turkey, *Monthly Statistics.*

Table K. **Dollar exchange rate of the Turkish lira**

TL per $

7th September 1946	2.80		1981 (annual average)	110.16
23rd August 1960	9.00		Q1	93.67
10th August 1970	14.85		Q2	101.99
28th December 1971	14.00		Q3	117.85
16th February 1973	13.85		Q4	127.13
15th August 1973	14.00		1982 (annual average)	160.76
14th May 1974	13.50		Q1	140.83
20th September 1974	13.85		Q2	151.54
17th April 1975	14.00		Q3	169.83
8th July 1975	14.25		Q4	180.86
8th August 1975	14.50		1983 (annual average)	223.80
28th August 1975	14.75		Q1	192.51
28th October 1975	15.00		Q2	210.81
15th March 1976	15.50		Q3	233.06
4th April 1976	16.00		Q4	258.83
27th October 1976	16.50		1984 (annual average)	364.85
1st March 1977	17.50		Q1	307.41
21st September 1977	19.25		Q2	341.15
1st March 1978	25.00		Q3	385.87
10th April 1979	26.50	(47.10)[1]	Q4	419.44
10th May 1979	26.50	(42.10)[1]	1985 (annual average)	518.34
10th June 1979	47.10[2]		Q1	468.23
25th January 1980	70.00	(55.00)[3]	Q2	516.48
2nd April 1980	73.70	(57.90)[3]	Q3	536.02
9th June 1980	78.00	(61.30)[3]	Q4	556.51
4th August 1980	80.00	(62.87)[3]	1986 (annual average)	669.03
11th October 1980	82.70	(65.19)[3]	Q1	598.51
26th October 1980	84.80	(72.50)[3]	Q2	666.40
9th November 1980	87.95	(77.50)[3]	Q3	676.87
10th December 1980	89.25	(78.66)[3]	Q4	733.95
27th January 1981	91.90	(79.41)[3]	1987	
5th February 1981	95.95	(83.38)[3]	Q1	760.32
24th March 1981	95.65	(83.12)[3]		
15th April 1981	98.20			
May 1981	101.92[4]			

1. Premium rate for workers' remittances and tourism revenues.
2. For exports of traditional agricultural goods and imports of petroleum and its products and fertilizer raw materials $ parity is kept at TL 35.00.
3. For imports of fertilizer and agricultural pesticides.
4. Since 1st May 1981, the exchange rate has been adjusted on a daily basis. The figures shown are averages of the daily exchange rates.

Source: Central Bank of Turkey, *Monthly Statistics.*

Table L. **External debt of Turkey**[1]

Disbursed debt – End of period

$ million

	1981	1982	1983	1984	1985	1986[2]
Medium- and long-term debt	14 667	15 855	16 104	18 078	20 590	24 317
Multilateral organisations	3 857	4 531	4 916	5 494	6 157	6 588
IMF	1 322	1 455	1 572	1 426	1 326	1 085
World Bank, IDA, IFC	1 783	2 115	2 488	3 044	3 470	3 643
European Investment Bank	427	420	393	391	429	573
European Resettlement Fund	287	384	399	554	801	1 197
Islamic Development Bank	23	117	22	35	35	53
OPEC Fund	15	40	40	40	35	29
International Fund for Agricultural Development	–	–	2	4	7	8
Bilateral credits	6 712	7 115	6 560	7 204	7 955	10 187
OECD countries	5 901	6 146	5 607	5 987	6 528	8 270
OPEC countries	449	587	535	603	640	1 027
Other countries	362	382	418	614	787	890
Commercial banks	3 257	3 229	3 262	3 704	4 351	4 833
Rescheduled debt	2 606	2 509	2 360	2 081	1 973	. .
Guaranteed credits	95	15	7	177	417	. .
Non-guaranteed credits	556	705	895	1 446	1 961	. .
Private lenders	841	980	1 366	1 676	2 127	2 709
Dresdner Bank scheme	. .	400	758	1 326	1 858	2 480
Others	841	580	608	350	269	229
Short-term debt	2 194	1 764	2 278	3 180	4 759	6 911
Bankers credits	–	–	65	195	432	944
Overdrafts	69	48	164	417	376	77
Acceptance credits	230	276	318	703	1 093	1 061
Prefinancing credits	330	199	254	414	609	629
CTLDs	473	585	647	61	18	6
Dresdner Bank scheme	472	417	493	452	820	1 308
Other foreign currency deposits	–	–	83	544	724	1 250
Other	620	239	248	394	687	1 636
Total debt	16 861	17 619	18 385	21 258	25 349	31 228

1. Excluding military debt and debt under trade arrangements with some Eastern European countries.
2. Provisional.

Source: Central Bank of Turkey, *Annual Report.*

Table M. **General government consolidated account**

TL billion

	1965	1970	1975	1980	1981	1982	1983	1984	1985
Revenues	14.6	35.9	137.8	1 114.5	1 737.2	2 165.3	2 986.8	3 890.6	6 406.6
1. *Tax revenues*	11.3	25.2	98.3	789.1	1 244.6	1 592.0	2 048.9	2 682.1	4 544.6
Central government	10.3	23.0	95.0	749.8	1 190.2	1 522.3	1 934.5	2 372.1	3 829.1
Local administrations	1.0	2.2	3.3	39.3	54.4	69.7	114.4	234.9	438.8
Special funds	–	–	–	–	–	–	–	75.1	276.7
2. *Social security premiums*	1.1	4.6	23.1	138.3	207.6	288.2	397.0	568.2	805.8
3. *Non-tax revenues*	2.2	6.1	16.4	187.1	285.0	285.1	540.9	640.3	1 056.2
Central government	1.3	4.9	12.7	163.6	208.2	174.7	379.5	433.5	647.0
Local administrations	0.9	0.5	1.9	5.2	48.4	62.8	90.5	75.7	201.0
Social security institutions	0.0	0.7	1.8	18.3	28.4	47.6	70.9	131.1	129.1
Special funds	–	–	–	–	–	–	–	–	79.1
Expenditures	16.1	36.7	131.8	1 264.3	1 786.6	2 307.6	3 203.9	4 586.8	6 833.0
1. *Current expenditures*	8.5	17.0	62.3	522.1	670.6	904.0	1 183.2	1 653.2	2 367.6
(Personnel)	(..)	(5.4)	(32.2)	(389.5)	(446.5)	(636.4)	(744.1)	(1 023.7)	(1 440.8)
Central government	7.6	14.7	56.5	463.8	602.8	823.0	1 062.0	1 484.0	2 086.0
Local administrations	0.9	1.9	4.8	50.8	58.9	69.5	106.5	149.4	245.3
Social security institutions	0.0	0.4	1.0	7.5	8.9	11.5	14.7	19.8	27.5
Special funds	–	–	–	–	–	–	–	–	8.8
2. *Investment expenditures*	4.1	7.9	28.0	255.9	410.0	531.7	586.6	833.5	1 456.6
Central government	3.5	7.0	25.3	219.9	359.8	463.8	478.0	688.0	989.0
Local administrations	0.6	0.9	2.6	35.0	48.6	66.9	105.5	136.7	294.2
Social security institutions	0.0	0.0	0.1	1.0	1.6	2.0	3.1	5.4	5.8
Special funds	–	–	–	–	–	–	–	3.4	167.6
3. *Transfer expenditures*	3.5	11.8	41.5	486.8	706.0	870.9	1 434.1	2 100.1	3 008.8
Central government	3.0	7.1	26.1	344.2	493.3	563.9	959.1	1 440.3	1 947.7
Local administrations	0.3	0.7	1.2	5.3	2.8	5.0	21.7	28.8	74.7
Social security institutions	0.2	4.0	14.2	136.8	209.9	302.0	453.3	630.7	947.2
Special funds	–	–	–	–	–	–	–	0.3	39.2
Balance	–1.5	–0.8	6.0	–149.8	–49.4	–142.3	–217.1	–696.2	–426.4

Source: OECD Secretariat calculations based on data submitted by the Turkish authorities.

Table N. **Central government budget**

TL billion

	1965	1970	1975	1980	1981	1982	1983	1984	1985
Revenues	11.6	27.9	107.7	913.5	1 398.4	1 697.0	2 314.0	2 840.0	4 476.1
Tax revenues	10.3	23.0	95.0	749.9	1 190.2	1 522.3	1 934.5	2 372.1	3 829.1
Non-tax revenues	1.3	4.9	12.7	163.6	208.2	174.7	379.5	467.9	647.0
Expenditures	14.1	30.8	112.9	1 078.3	1 515.6	1 922.0	2 612.5	3 784.0	5 263.0
Current expenditures	7.6	14.7	56.5	463.8	602.8	823.0	1 062.0	1 484.0	2 086.0
Personnel	..	4.2	31.2	351.0	405.0	588.0	671.0	925.0	1 275.0
Investment	3.5	7.0	25.3	219.9	359.8	463.0	478.0	688.0	989.0
Transfers	3.0	9.1	31.1	394.6	553.0	636.0	1 072.5	1 612.0	2 188.0
of which:									
SEEs	0.8	2.0	10.0	174.7	191.4	223.9	302.0	274.6	180.7
Interest payments	0.4	0.9	3.2	28.2	67.4	92.9	181.0	375.0	595.0
Balance	–2.5	–2.9	–5.2	–164.8	–117.2	–225.0	–298.4	–944.0	–786.9
Borrowing	2.2	4.5	7.4	42.3	69.9	151.0	257.9	764.1	867.0
Domestic	1.0	1.5	–	17.4	22.6	108.0	198.5	194.8	670.0
Foreign	1.2	3.0	7.4	24.9	47.3	43.0	59.4	569.3	197.0
Repayments	–0.5	–1.4	–3.4	–37.2	–49.1	–105.6	–179.8	–293.7	–592.0
Domestic	..	–0.9	–2.0	–30.0	–26.9	–40.8	–30.0	–57.8	–172.0
Foreign	..	–0.5	–1.4	–7.2	–22.2	–64.8	–149.8	–235.9	–420.0
Short-term borrowing (net)	0.8	–0.2	1.2	159.9	96.4	179.6	220.3	508.0	511.9
Central Bank	0.5	0.0	0.0	103.0	39.0	32.0	72.0	190.0	266.0
Treasury Bills	–	1.9	1.2	56.9	57.4	64.5	148.3	284.0	244.0
Change in bank cash (– increase)	0.3	–2.1	–	–	–	83.1	–	56.0	1.9

Source: Secretariat calculations based on data submitted by the Turkish authorities.

Table O. **Local administrations**

TL billion

	1965	1970	1975	1980	1981	1982	1983	1984	1985
Revenues	1.9	3.7	7.8	66.3	120.1	150.5	234.3	357.5	663.3
Tax revenues	1.0	2.2	3.3	39.3	54.4	69.7	114.4	234.9	438.8
Direct	0.4	1.4	1.5	22.2	29.8	33.0	55.7	113.3	208.9
Indirect	0.6	0.8	1.8	17.1	24.6	36.7	58.7	211.6	229.9
Other revenues	0.9	1.5	4.5	27.0	65.7	80.8	119.9	122.6	224.5
Expenditures	1.8	3.5	8.6	91.1	110.3	141.1	233.7	314.9	614.2
Current	0.9	1.9	4.8	50.8	58.9	69.5	106.5	149.4	245.3
(Personnel)	(0.2)	(1.2)	(3.7)	(38.5)	(41.5)	(48.4)	(73.1)	(98.7)	(157.1)
Investment	0.6	0.9	2.6	35.0	48.6	66.6	105.5	136.7	294.2
Transfers	0.3	0.7	1.2	5.3	2.8	5.0	21.7	28.8	74.7
Balance	0.1	0.2	0.8	–24.8	9.8	9.4	0.6	42.6	49.1
Transfers from budget	0.0	1.0	2.6	21.8	17.3	18.0	29.4	46.4	23.5
Net revenues	1.9	2.7	5.2	44.5	102.8	132.5	204.9	310.6	639.8

Source: OECD Secretariat calculations based on data submitted by the Turkish authorities.

Table P. **Social security institutions: Pension Fund, Social Insurance Agency, Bag-Kur**

TL billion

	1965	1970	1975	1980	1981	1982	1983	1984	1985
I. **Revenues**	1.1	6.0	27.3	177.9	278.4	387.6	551.9	824.1	1 151.7
1. *Social security premiums*	1.1	4.6	23.1	138.3	207.6	288.2	397.0	568.2	805.8
Pension Fund	0.5	1.6	9.6	43.0	56.0	79.8	98.1	130.4	163.9
Social insurance	0.6	3.0	13.5	86.8	139.9	190.1	275.4	403.3	572.4
Bag-Kur	–	–		7.9	11.7	18.3	23.5	34.5	69.5
2. *Other revenues*	0.0	1.4	4.2	39.6	70.8	99.4	154.9	259.9	345.9
Pension Fund	0.0	0.7	2.1	26.1	48.4	61.5	98.4	147.8	245.2
Social insurance	0.0	0.7	2.1	13.5	22.3	37.8	56.4	108.0	100.6
Bag-Kur	–	–	0.0	0.0	0.1	0.1	0.1	0.1	0.1
II. **Expenditures**	0.3	4.4	15.3	145.3	220.4	315.5	471.2	655.9	980.5
1. *Current expenditures*	0.1	0.4	1.0	7.5	8.9	11.5	14.7	19.8	27.5
Pension Fund	0.1	0.1	0.2	1.4	1.7	2.2	2.9	4.3	6.3
Social insurance	0.0	0.3	0.8	6.1	7.2	9.3	11.8	15.5	21.2
Bag-Kur	–	–	–	–	–	–	–	–	–
2. *Investment expenditures*	0.0	0.0	0.1	1.0	1.6	2.0	3.1	5.4	5.8
Pension Fund	0.0	0.0	0.0	0.3	0.4	0.5	1.3	1.1	1.0
Social insurance	0.0	0.0	0.1	0.7	1.2	1.5	1.8	4.2	4.5
Bag-Kur	–	–	–	–	–	–	0.0	0.1	0.3
3. *Social security transfers*	0.2	4.0	14.2	136.8	209.9	302.0	453.4	630.7	947.2
Pension Fund	0.0	1.7	6.6	61.9	98.8	138.3	187.3	266.7	399.4
Social insurance	0.2	2.3	7.6	70.8	103.6	152.6	245.3	332.0	499.4
Bag-Kur	–	–	0.0	4.1	7.6	11.1	20.8	32.0	48.8
Balance	0.9	1.6	12.0	32.6	58.0	72.1	80.7	168.2	171.2
Transfers from budget	0.0	0.7	2.4	21.4	42.4	51.8	84.0	124.8	216.8
Net revenues	1.1	5.3	24.9	156.5	236.0	335.8	467.9	699.3	934.9

Source: OECD Secretariat calculations based on data submitted by the Turkish authorities.

Table Q. **Special funds: Revenues and expenditures**

TL billion

	1984	1985	1986[1]
Housing Fund	69.5	183.6	283.3
Revenues	73.2	192.6	324.3
Expenditures	3.7	10.0	41.0
Public Participation Fund	–	–43.2	–332.5
Revenues		79.0	202.9
Expenditures		122.2	535.4
Support and Development Fund	1.9	19.2	41.7
Revenues	1.9	60.4	124.9
Expenditures	–	41.2	83.2
Petroleum Consumption Fund	–	1.3	–1.4
Revenues		52.0	91.9
Expenditures		50.7	93.3
Defence Industry Fund	–	–	142.3
Revenues			166.5
Expenditures			24.2
Tax Administration Fund	–	–	25.3
Revenues			37.5
Expenditures			12.2
Social Solidarity Fund	–	–	1.5
Revenues			77.9
Expenditures			76.4
Support and Price Stability Fund	–	–	26.9
Revenues			182.3
Expenditures			155.4
Total revenues[2]	75.1	376.5	1 175.3
Total expenditures[2]	3.7	215.6	986.8
Funds' balance	71.4	160.9	188.5

1. Provisional.
2. Totals are net of inter-fund transfers. Borrowing by the funds and credits extended are not included in revenues or expenditures.

Source: OECD Secretariat calculations based on data submitted by the Turkish authorities.

BASIC STATISTICS : INTERNATIONAL COMPARISONS

	Units	Reference period[1]	Australia	Austr
Population				
Total	Thousands	1985	15 752	7 555
Inhabitants per sq.km	Number		2	90
Net average annual increase over previous 10 years	%		1.3	0.0
Employment				
Total civilian employment (TCE)[2]	Thousands	1985	6 676	3 235
of which: Agriculture	% of TCE		6.2	9.0
Industry	% of TCE		27.7	38.1
Services	% of TCE		66.1	52.9
Gross domestic product (GDP)				
At current prices and current exchange rates	Billion US$	1985	155.1	66.1
Per capita	US$		9 847	8 743
At current prices using current PPP's[3]	Billion US$	1984	..	85.7
Per capita	US$		..	11 345
Average annual volume growth over previous 5 years	%	1985	3.0	1.6
Gross fixed capital formation (GFCF)	% of GDP	1985	24.4	22.3
of which: Machinery and equipment	% of GDP		10.4 (84)	9.6
Residential construction	% of GDP		5.4 (84)	4.6
Average annual volume growth over previous 5 years	%	1984	1.9	–0.5
Gross saving ratio[4]	% of GDP	1985	20.1	24.4
General government				
Current expenditure on goods and services	% of GDP	1985	16.7	18.7
Current disbursements[5]	% of GDP	1985	33.4 (84)	44.9 (
Current receipts	% of GDP	1985	34.1 (84)	47.0 (
Net official development assistance	% of GNP	1984	0.46	0.28
Indicators of living standards				
Private consumption per capita using current PPP's[3]	US$	1984	6 742 *	6 490
Passenger cars, per 1 000 inhabitants	Number	1985	..	306 (
Telephones, per 1 000 inhabitants	Number	1985	540 (83)	460 (
Television sets, per 1 000 inhabitants	Number	1985	..	300 (
Doctors, per 1 000 inhabitants	Number	1985	..	1.7 (
Infant mortality per 1 000 live births	Number	1985	9.2 (84)	11.0
Wages and prices (average annual increase over previous 5 years)				
Wages (earnings or rates according to availability)	%	1986	7.7	5.0
Consumer prices	%	1986	8.2	3.8
Foreign trade				
Exports of goods, fob*	Million US$	1986	22 536	22 428
as % of GDP	%		14.5	33.9
average annual increase over previous 5 years	%		0.7	7.3
Imports of goods, cif*	Million US$	1986	23 916	26 724
as % of GDP	%		15.4	40.4
average annual increase over previous 5 years	%		0.1	4.9
Total official reserves[6]	Million SDR's	1986	6 202	5 778
As ratio of average monthly imports of goods	Ratio		3.7	3.0

* At current prices and exchange rates.
1. Unless otherwise stated.
2. According to the definitions used in OECD *Labour force Statistics*.
3. PPP's = Purchasing Power Parities.
4. Gross saving = Gross national disposable income *minus* Private and Government consumption.
5. Current disbursements = Current expenditure on goods and services *plus* current transfers and payments of property income.
6. Gold included in reserves is valued at 35 SDR's per ounce. End of year.
7. Including Luxembourg.
8. Included in Belgium.
9. Including non-residential construction.

EMPLOYMENT OPPORTUNITIES

Economics and Statistics Department

OECD

A. **Administrator.** A number of economist positions may become available in 1987 in areas such as monetary and fiscal policy, balance of payments, resource allocation, macroeconomic policy issues, short-term forecasting and country studies. *Essential* qualifications and experience: advanced university degree in economics; good knowledge of statistical methods and applied econometrics; two or three years' experience in applied economic analysis; command of one of the two official languages (English and French). *Desirable* qualifications and experience also include: familiarity with the economic problems and data sources of a number of Member countries; proven drafting ability; experience with the estimation, simulation and implementation of computer-based economic models; some knowledge of the other official language.

B. **Principal Administrator.** A number of senior economist positions may become available in 1987 in areas such as monetary and fiscal policy, balance of payments, resource allocation, macroeconomic policy issues, short-term forecasting and country studies. *Essential* qualifications and experience: advanced university degree in economics; extensive experience in applied economic analysis, preferably with a central bank, economics/finance ministry or institute of economic research; good knowledge of statistical methods and applied econometrics; command of one of the two official languages (English and French) and proven drafting ability. *Desirable* qualifications and experience also include: experience in using economic analysis for formulating policy advice; familiarity with a number of OECD economies; experience in using econometric models; good knowledge of the other official language.

These positions carry a basic salary (tax free) from FF 193 968 or FF 239 328 (Administrator) and from FF 275 412 (Principal Administrator), supplemented by further additional allowances depending on residence and family situation.

Initial appointment will be on a two- or three-year fixed-term contract.

Vacancies are open to both male and female candidates from OECD Member countries. Applications citing reference "ECSUR", together with a detailed curriculum vitæ in English or French, should be sent to:

Head of Personnel
OECD
2, rue André-Pascal
75775 PARIS CEDEX 16
France

OECD SALES AGENTS
DÉPOSITAIRES DES PUBLICATIONS DE L'OCDE

ARGENTINA - ARGENTINE
Carlos Hirsch S.R.L.,
Florida 165, 4° Piso,
(Galeria Guemes) 1333 Buenos Aires
Tel. 33.1787.2391 y 30.7122

AUSTRALIA-AUSTRALIE
D.A. Book (Aust.) Pty. Ltd.
11-13 Station Street (P.O. Box 163)
Mitcham, Vic. 3132 Tel. (03) 873 4411

AUSTRIA - AUTRICHE
OECD Publications and Information Centre,
4 Simrockstrasse,
5300 Bonn (Germany) Tel. (0228) 21.60.45
Local Agent:
Gerold & Co., Graben 31, Wien 1 Tel. 52.22.35

BELGIUM - BELGIQUE
Jean de Lannoy, Service Publications OCDE,
avenue du Roi 202
B-1060 Bruxelles Tel. (02) 538.51.69

CANADA
Renouf Publishing Company Ltd/
Éditions Renouf Ltée,
1294 Algoma Road, Ottawa, Ont. K1B 3W8
Tel: (613) 741-4333
Toll Free/Sans Frais:
Ontario, Quebec, Maritimes:
1-800-267-1805
Western Canada, Newfoundland:
1-800-267-1826
Stores/Magasins:
61 rue Sparks St., Ottawa, Ont. K1P 5A6
Tel: (613) 238-8985
211 rue Yonge St., Toronto, Ont. M5B 1M4
Tel: (416) 363-3171
Sales Office/Bureau des Ventes:
7575 Trans Canada Hwy, Suite 305,
St. Laurent, Quebec H4T 1V6
Tel: (514) 335-9274

DENMARK - DANEMARK
Munksgaard Export and Subscription Service
35, Nørre Søgade, DK-1370 København K
Tel. +45.1.12.85.70

FINLAND - FINLANDE
Akateeminen Kirjakauppa,
Keskuskatu 1, 00100 Helsinki 10 Tel. 0.12141

FRANCE
OCDE/OECD
Mail Orders/Commandes par correspondance :
2, rue André-Pascal,
75775 Paris Cedex 16
Tel. (1) 45.24.82.00
Bookshop/Librairie : 33, rue Octave-Feuillet
75016 Paris
Tel. (1) 45.24.81.67 or/ou (1) 45.24.81.81
Principal correspondant :
Librairie de l'Université,
12*a*, rue Nazareth,
13602 Aix-en-Provence Tel. 42.26.18.08

GERMANY - ALLEMAGNE
OECD Publications and Information Centre,
4 Simrockstrasse,
5300 Bonn Tel. (0228) 21.60.45

GREECE - GRÈCE
Librairie Kauffmann,
28, rue du Stade, 105 64 Athens Tel. 322.21.60

HONG KONG
Government Information Services,
Publications (Sales) Office,
Beaconsfield House, 4/F.,
Queen's Road Central

ICELAND - ISLANDE
Snæbjörn Jónsson & Co., h.f.,
Hafnarstræti 4 & 9,
P.O.B. 1131 – Reykjavik
Tel. 13133/14281/11936

INDIA - INDE
Oxford Book and Stationery Co.,
Scindia House, New Delhi I Tel. 331.5896/5308
17 Park St., Calcutta 700016 Tel. 240832

INDONESIA - INDONÉSIE
Pdii-Lipi, P.O. Box 3065/JKT.Jakarta
Tel. 583467

IRELAND - IRLANDE
TDC Publishers - Library Suppliers,
12 North Frederick Street, Dublin 1.
Tel. 744835-749677

ITALY - ITALIE
Libreria Commissionaria Sansoni,
Via Lamarmora 45, 50121 Firenze
Tel. 579751/584468
Via Bartolini 29, 20155 Milano Tel. 365083
Sub-depositari :
Editrice e Libreria Herder,
Piazza Montecitorio 120, 00186 Roma
Tel. 6794628
Libreria Hœpli,
Via Hœpli 5, 20121 Milano Tel. 865446
Libreria Scientifica
Dott. Lucio de Biasio "Aeiou"
Via Meravigli 16, 20123 Milano Tel. 807679
Libreria Lattes,
Via Garibaldi 3, 10122 Torino Tel. 519274
La diffusione delle edizioni OCSE è inoltre assicurata dalle migliori librerie nelle città più importanti.

JAPAN - JAPON
OECD Publications and Information Centre,
Landic Akasaka Bldg., 2-3-4 Akasaka,
Minato-ku, Tokyo 107 Tel. 586.2016

KOREA - CORÉE
Kyobo Book Centre Co. Ltd.
P.O.Box: Kwang Hwa Moon 1658,
Seoul Tel. (REP) 730.78.91

LEBANON - LIBAN
Documenta Scientifica/Redico,
Edison Building, Bliss St.,
P.O.B. 5641, Beirut Tel. 354429-344425

MALAYSIA - MALAISIE
University of Malaya Co-operative Bookshop
Ltd.,
P.O.Box 1127, Jalan Pantai Baru,
Kuala Lumpur Tel. 577701/577072

NETHERLANDS - PAYS-BAS
Staatsuitgeverij
Chr. Plantijnstraat, 2 Postbus 20014
2500 EA S-Gravenhage Tel. 070-789911
Voor bestellingen: Tel. 070-789880

NEW ZEALAND - NOUVELLE-ZÉLANDE
Government Printing Office Bookshops:
Auckland: Retail Bookshop, 25 Rutland Street,
Mail Orders, 85 Beach Road
Private Bag C.P.O.
Hamilton: Retail: Ward Street,
Mail Orders, P.O. Box 857
Wellington: Retail, Mulgrave Street, (Head Office)
Cubacade World Trade Centre,
Mail Orders, Private Bag
Christchurch: Retail, 159 Hereford Street,
Mail Orders, Private Bag
Dunedin: Retail, Princes Street,
Mail Orders, P.O. Box 1104

NORWAY - NORVÈGE
Tanum-Karl Johan
Karl Johans gate 43, Oslo 1
PB 1177 Sentrum, 0107 Oslo 1Tel. (02) 42.93.10

PAKISTAN
Mirza Book Agency
65 Shahrah Quaid-E-Azam, Lahore 3 Tel. 66839

PORTUGAL
Livraria Portugal,
Rua do Carmo 70-74, 1117 Lisboa Codex.
Tel. 360582/3

SINGAPORE - SINGAPOUR
Information Publications Pte Ltd
Pei-Fu Industrial Building,
24 New Industrial Road No. 02-06
Singapore 1953 Tel. 2831786, 2831798

SPAIN - ESPAGNE
Mundi-Prensa Libros, S.A.,
Castelló 37, Apartado 1223, Madrid-28001
Tel. 431.33.99
Libreria Bosch, Ronda Universidad 11,
Barcelona 7 Tel. 317.53.08/317.53.58

SWEDEN - SUÈDE
AB CE Fritzes Kungl. Hovbokhandel,
Box 16356, S 103 27 STH,
Regeringsgatan 12,
DS Stockholm Tel. (08) 23.89.00
Subscription Agency/Abonnements:
Wennergren-Williams AB,
Box 30004, S104 25 Stockholm.
Tel. (08)54.12.00

SWITZERLAND - SUISSE
OECD Publications and Information Centre,
4 Simrockstrasse,
5300 Bonn (Germany) Tel. (0228) 21.60.45
Local Agent:
Librairie Payot,
6 rue Grenus, 1211 Genève 11
Tel. (022) 31.89.50

TAIWAN - FORMOSE
Good Faith Worldwide Int'l Co., Ltd.
9th floor, No. 118, Sec.2
Chung Hsiao E. Road
Taipei Tel. 391.7396/391.7397

THAILAND - THAILANDE
Suksit Siam Co., Ltd.,
1715 Rama IV Rd.,
Samyam Bangkok 5 Tel. 2511630

TURKEY - TURQUIE
Kültur Yayinlari Is-Türk Ltd. Sti.
Atatürk Bulvari No: 191/Kat. 21
Kavaklidere/Ankara Tel. 25.07.60
Dolmabahce Cad. No: 29
Besiktas/Istanbul Tel. 160.71.88

UNITED KINGDOM - ROYAUME-UNI
H.M. Stationery Office,
Postal orders only: (01)211-5656
P.O.B. 276, London SW8 5DT
Telephone orders: (01) 622.3316, or
Personal callers:
49 High Holborn, London WC1V 6HB
Branches at: Belfast, Birmingham,
Bristol, Edinburgh, Manchester

UNITED STATES - ÉTATS-UNIS
OECD Publications and Information Centre,
2001 L Street, N.W., Suite 700,
Washington, D.C. 20036 - 4095
Tel. (202) 785.6323

VENEZUELA
Libreria del Este,
Avda F. Miranda 52, Aptdo. 60337,
Edificio Galipan, Caracas 106
Tel. 32.23.01/33.26.04/31.58.38

YUGOSLAVIA - YOUGOSLAVIE
Jugoslovenska Knjiga, Knez Mihajlova 2,
P.O.B. 36, Beograd Tel. 621.992

Orders and inquiries from countries where Sales Agents have not yet been appointed should be sent to:
OECD, Publications Service, Sales and Distribution Division, 2, rue André-Pascal, 75775 PARIS CEDEX 16.

Les commandes provenant de pays où l'OCDE n'a pas encore désigné de dépositaire peuvent être adressées à :
OCDE, Service des Publications. Division des Ventes et Distribution. 2. rue André-Pascal. 75775 PARIS CEDEX 16.

70712-04-1987

OECD PUBLICATIONS
2, rue André-Pascal
75775 PARIS CEDEX 16
No. 43993
(10 87 27 1) ISBN 92-64-12977-4
ISSN 0376-6438

PRINTED IN FRANCE